1001 Dreams

An illustrated guide to dreams and their meanings

Jack Altman

DUNCAN BAIRD PUBLISHERS

LONDON

1001 Dreams
Jack Altman

First published in the US by Chronicle Books

Conceived, created and designed by
Duncan Baird Publishers Ltd
Sixth Floor
Castle House
75–76 Wells Street
London W1T 3QH

Editors: Judy Barratt, Peter Bently, Hanne
Bewernick, James Hodgson, Christopher Westhorp
Designer: Gail Jones
Commissioned artwork: Joanna Eastbury,
Emma Harding

British Library Cataloguing-in-Publication Data:
A CIP record for this book is available from the
British Library

ISBN: 1-904292-13-5

10 9 8 7 6

Typeset in Shannon
Colour reproduction by Scanhouse, Malaysia
Printed and bound in Thailand by Imago

CONTENTS

FOREWORD

Psychological theories of dreams can be divided into two groups. The first sees dreams simply as the brain processing and dumping unwanted mental material at the end of the day, rather as the computer discards unwanted data before shutting down. The second maintains that, correctly interpreted, dreams give valuable insights into our unconscious minds. After more than 25 years working with dreams in many areas of psychology, I have no doubt that the second group of theories is correct. Each of us dreams a total of approximately two hours every night, and with practice these dreams can be recalled and studied to give us deeper and more comprehensive self-understanding.

Of course, not everything in dreams reveals amazing secrets. The dreaming mind conducts fantasies, just as when day-dreaming. But much of the dream is constructed around themes that reveal our hopes and fears, disappointments and aspirations, often reaching back into childhood memories to do so. And because dreams involve brain areas that evolved before language, much of their meaning takes symbolic rather than verbal form. Many of these symbols are personal to the dreamer, which means that the dogmatic interpretations given in dream dictionaries can be actively misleading. For this reason, *1001 Dreams* offers instead well-researched guidelines which help you identify meaning for yourself. In doing so it captures much of the colour and excitement of dreams. Reading it will help bring a new dimension to your dream life, and enable you to probe more deeply into the fascinating mysteries of your own mind.

Professor David Fontana

INTRODUCTION

Many people have sought to understand the astonishing array of vivid images produced by the sleeping brain, from ancient philosophers, religious sages and students of esoterica to psychoanalysts, psychologists and brain scientists. The meanings suggested for the 1001 dreams listed here draw upon the approaches of various experienced observers of the dream phenomenon, notably – but by no means exclusively – the two giants in this field, Freud and Jung. Freud famously called dreams "the royal road to the unconscious" and his dream interpretations – indeed his whole psychoanalytical approach – emphasized unconscious desires, especially sexual ones, while Jung based his approach on the concept of a "collective unconscious" and universal "archetypes". Modern dream theorists draw upon the legacy of these two figures and that of their successors as well as ongoing discoveries about the intricate workings of the brain.

No single interpretation of dreams can satisfy everyone. For example, some people may be disappointed that this book avoids the idea that dreams predict future events – an approach that formed the basis of much dream-interpretation before Freud. Perhaps the least controversial thing that can be said about dreams is that they arise directly from our own lives – our thoughts, our emotions and our encounters with the world about us. Whatever experts suggest about our dreams, in the end we must decide for ourselves which interpretations we find most convincing, based on our own individual experiences.

THE FREUDIAN VIEW

Dreams provided Sigmund Freud (1856–1939) with the basic raw material for his revolutionary theories of psychoanalysis. A medically-trained physician in Vienna, Freud introduced his ideas in the historic work *The Interpretation of Dreams* (1899). Dreams, he claimed, functioned as a form of wish-fulfilment, acting out in fantastic or symbolic form the desires buried in his patients' unconscious minds. The book describes how, in particular, unresolved childhood emotional issues that lie repressed in the unconscious can be expressed through dreams.

Freud distinguished the dream's "manifest content" – the overt subject-matter that the dreamer recalls on waking – from its "latent content" – revealed under psychoanalysis. The method that Freud advocated for drawing the latent content out of the unconscious and into the light of the conscious mind was "free association". Under analysis, his patients recalled their dream and then expressed spontaneously anything that was evoked by the subject-matter. However irrelevant they seemed at first, these associations might lead to an understanding of the dreamer's deepest preoccupations.

For Freud, there are three categories of dreams. In the most basic wish-fulfilment dreams, such as those of children, the manifest and latent content coincide. The subject-matter of a dream provides a clear, direct indication of its sense: a dream of cherries or cake is simply a wish

for cherries or cake, particularly when they have been forbidden. In the second category, the dream's content is also
straightforward and its meaning therefore perfectly clear –
but the content itself is astonishing because we cannot in
our conscious state imagine such an idea. It may be a desire to
do something that we have never previously contemplated.

The manifest content in Freud's third category of dreams is obscure,
absurd and incoherent – for example, familiar figures performing incongruous actions in a strange environment. To understand the dream's
enigmas, we have to dig deep into an uncomfortable underlying content
that many people are reluctant to examine.

Freud notes several methods by which wishes are disguised, hidden
or repressed in dreams so that the sleeper cannot easily recognize their
true meaning on waking. One process is the **transformation** of abstract
concepts into recognizable images and situations. An adult's yearning
for the pleasures of childhood and the tenderness of the mother,
prompted by a desire for affection that is absent from their present life,
may be revealed, according to Freud, in a dream of mountains of cake.

Another process is **condensation**, in which several elements combine
into one complex image. A dream of a proud and stern old soldier
might represent both the dreamer's father and the psychoanalyst perceived as an authoritarian father-figure.

A third process, **displacement**, translates the dreamer's crucial latent thoughts and feelings into terms that may seem insignificant or irrelevant. Thus what may seem like an unremarkable dream of sitting for a long time in a train that does not move may reveal the dreamer's serious frustrations with his or her marriage.

The most obvious means by which our dreaming minds disguise our true feelings is the use of **symbolism**. For Freud, the process of replacing people, objects, actions and feelings with symbolic images enables dreamers to express their unconscious desires in a palatable and apparently unintelligible form. He argues that sleep might be impossible if this "censorship" did not make it easier for dreamers to deal with their darkest desires. The symbols become all the more obscure and impenetrable when the repressed desires are ones that would be considered morally unacceptable in the dreamer's waking life – such as incest or murder.

Resistance to Freud's dream analysis has focused on what many consider an overemphasis on sex. For example, few modern psychologists believe in the "Oedipus complex", Freud's theory of a son's supposed attraction to his mother and rivalry and hostility toward his father. In a young girl the equivalent process is weaker and is known as the "Electra complex", which manifests itself in a girl's desire for her father. (In Greek myth, Oedipus was separated from his parents at birth; later, before he discovered their identities, he killed his father and married his mother.)

Freudian analysts who now attribute significance to other social and cultural influences (as did Freud himself in later life) still ascribe a major role to sexuality in the unconscious. They also suggest that the discomfort many feel about Freud's approach reflects, unconsciously, their repression of unacceptable but still perhaps valid interpretations.

THE JUNGIAN VIEW

Like Freud, the Swiss-born psychotherapist Carl Gustav Jung (1875–1961) appreciated the key place of the unconscious in his patients' psychological problems and the vital role of dreams in revealing the sources of these problems. Jung had begun to develop a different approach from Freud even before the two met in 1907. Nevertheless, seven years of close collaboration followed before Jung decided to work independently. Jung disagreed most with Freud's insistence that each patient's dreams were the fruit solely of his or her individual and personal conscious and unconscious experiences. Jung had observed that his patients' dreams shared many common motifs, and through his study of comparative religion, mythology and alchemy, he postulated that these motifs were to be found in all cultures and in all ages of humanity. They formed part of what he termed humankind's "collective unconscious".

In his *Symbols of Transformation* (1912), Jung describes the "supra-individual universality" of the collective unconscious as the source of human psychological life. Jungians believe that there is a "bank" of mythic ideas and motifs genetically inherited by all men and women. Jung referred to these inherited universal motifs, which he saw cropping up repeatedly in his patients' dreams in one form or another, as "archetypes". This wide range of motifs for which Jung had found parallels in cultures across the world, included figures such as "Wise Old Man",

"Great Mother", "Trickster" and "Divine Child" (see pages 15–17). The archetypes are also said to exist in individuals – according to Jung, a child's view of a father as hero and tyrant derives from universal archetypes he referred to as "Superman" and "Ogre". Archetypes appeared in what Jung called "grand dreams" arising from the collective unconscious. These, he believed, could open up a perspective into "the vast historical storehouse of the human race".

One of the most important factors in Jung's break with Freud was the latter's preoccupation with repressed childhood traumas and his insistence on a sexual analysis of "parent and child" dreams. Jung preferred to interpret such dreams through myth-related archetypes imprinted in the unconscious. Freud, of course, also saw the psychological complexity of myths and drew upon them (especially the classical mythic heritage of ancient Greece and Rome) to develop his psychoanalytical approach – most famously with his interpretation of the Oedipus story.

The goal of the Jungian interpretation of dreams, and Jungian analysis generally, is self-realization and spiritual discovery. Relevant in this connection is Jung's observation of "the numerous connections between individual dream symbolism and medieval alchemy." As Jung pointed out, alchemy went far beyond the popular image of a vain materialistic pursuit of a means to transform lead into gold. It was, in fact, a metaphysical process, a spiritual quest to turn the base matter of psychological disorder into the gold of personal wholeness. Borrowing an alchemical term, Jung referred to this attainment of psychological wholeness as "individuation".

Jung rejected Freudian free association as a technique for interpreting dreams, preferring what he called "direct association". Jungians prefer to direct the patient's train of thought so that it does not stray too far from the original image. They claim that it is important not to forget the goal of "psychic wholeness" that is the fundamental aim of Jungian psychotherapy and dream analysis.

Nine of the most important archetypes were referred to by Jung as the "dominants". Such archetypal figures are said to impart to dreamers a feeling of "receiving wisdom" from an external source.

The **Wise Old Man** appears in dreams as a male authority figure – father, teacher, doctor, priest or master magician. Jung refers to this and other archetypes by the term *mana*, meaning that they can be a source of personal growth and energy. The Wise Old Man possesses powers that can be a force for both healing and destruction. His teaching can take the dreamer to a higher level of consciousness.

The archetypal antihero, the **Trickster** is a wild and amoral force wreaking havoc in an otherwise orderly society. He combines the bestial and the divine. With malicious cunning and sly pranks, the Trickster plays the self-mocking buffoon who apes the arrogance of authority – and the pretensions of the dreamer's ego. He may appear in dreams, as he does in mythologies around the world, as a monkey, fox, hare, clown or other mischievous and playful image.

Often represented in dreams by figures from classical mythology or more recent popular culture, the **Hero** is a *mana* personality that can provide an inspirational role model. However, dreamers may identify too closely with the Hero and lose sight of their own specific potential.

The **Persona** embodies the image we choose to present to society. A mask of convenience, it need not be harmful if it remains in touch with our more complex, truer, deeper self, revealed to those closest to us.

The **Shadow** is said to evoke the animal side of the personality, the brutish nature of human beings beneath their civilized veneer. According to Jung, this archetype often takes on the character of a classic villain or traitor, such as the Devil or Judas. Usually of the same sex as the dreamer, the figure may be a jealous sibling, like the biblical Cain or one of Cinderella's sisters. The Shadow may point to our need to deal with destructive forces in our own nature.

An important figure in many religions and mythologies, the **Divine Child** is seen by Jungians as a force for regeneration. Dreamers discover in this archetype a child's innocence and fragility at the moment of embarking on a process of self-transformation. An encounter with the child may temper the self-importance of the ego.

As human beings carry within each of them components of both sexes, so the **Anima** archetype expresses for the male dreamer feminine qualities of temperament, impulses and reactions which each man needs to integrate within himself. Typically represented by goddesses and famous heroines, such as Aphrodite (Venus) and Cleopatra, the Anima may guide dreamers toward areas of potential they had not dared to explore. Its counterpart, the **Animus**, is often symbolized by such mythical figures as Apollo and Ulysses but also by Amazon warriors. It expresses the masculine attributes needed to complete a woman's personality. Similarly, the Animus may help the female dreamer to draw on hitherto unrealized strengths and energies.

The figure of the **Great Mother** is one of the most powerful influences on psychological growth. This eternally ambivalent archetype may be celestial and virginal as in Christianity or earthly and fecund as in Oriental and polytheistic religions. Like the Wise Old Man, she has the power to create and destroy.

Note on cross-references: Throughout this book the reader will find boxes with cross-references to dreams on related subjects or themes. In each case, the dream that is the starting point is referred to by its number alone. The related dreams are referred to by title and page number.

OUR INNER LIVES

CHANGE AND TRANSITION

1 WAKING

The dream of waking and getting up when in fact the dreamer is still fast asleep may signal reluctance to face unfamiliar challenges at times of change – such as marriage or a new job. Then again, perhaps this disconcerting dream-state of false wakefulness is the mind's way of subverting the signs that we are about to wake up for real, thereby fulfilling what Freud himself described as the main purpose of all dreams – "prolonging sleep instead of waking up".

2 OBJECT COMING TO LIFE

Bizarre transformations of objects into living creatures (such as a table turning into a horse, or a bed into a herd of sheep) suggest that the dreamer feels able to release some hitherto untapped inner potential. If an object turns into a monster, this could be a warning from the unconscious not to antagonize others in the process of realizing your potential.

3 CHANGING SEASON OR TIME OF DAY

A sudden switch from winter to summer or from night to day may indicate a positive new development in the dreamer's life. On the other hand, a change in the opposite direction – summer turning to winter, or day to night – might point to the need to confront and deal with some potentially dangerous impulses.

4 UNFAMILIAR SURROUNDINGS

An alarmingly grotesque landscape suggests an unwillingness or inability to cope with the unfamiliar. However, friendly people beckoning into strange but intriguing buildings may point to the stimulation and satisfaction that a new opportunity, such as a change of job, may offer. A return to the comfort of a once-familiar environment – the classic experience of **déjà vu (5)** – is widely interpreted by Freudians and Jungians alike as a desire in troubled times to return to the womb.

DIRECTION AND IDENTITY

6 BRIDGE

A bridge marks the frontier between the comfortable present and the unpredictable future. Crossing the bridge indicates our ability to move forward – our underlying strength to cope with life's journey, especially in the face of difficult events such as divorce, a new job or moving home.

7 LABYRINTH OR MAZE

Jung saw the dark, enclosed labyrinth as a symbol of the tortuous depths of the unconscious, and a dream of entering a labyrinth as representing

a journey of self-discovery. A void at the heart of the labyrinth may suggest the emptiness of despair, but according to the circumstances could also symbolize the serene centre of our being. As in the Greek myth of Theseus, who penetrated the Labyrinth of Crete to slay the Minotaur, our personal descent into the unconscious may involve confronting impulses that threaten our well-being. Similar to a labyrinth but open to the light, a maze can reflect the difficulty of finding a direction to follow in life. No one can predict the future, so we may have to rely on our instincts. A **map or chart (8)** can reassure us that we are on the right path.

9 BEING LOST IN DENSE VEGETATION

Lost among towering trees or tall reeds, we may feel our progress to be impeded by insurmountable obstacles. As in the tale of Hansel and

Gretel that many of us will recall from childhood, this feeling might evoke a profound longing for the comfort of a mother.

10 DESTRUCTION AND RUIN

Images of destruction can relate to life-changes that quite literally break with the past. A house standing in ruins may convey the broken family that will be left by an imminent divorce; fallen trees can symbolize a family uprooted by emigration, exile or just a move to a new locality.

11 CAR LOSING CONTROL

Dreams of a vehicle careering out of control evoke worries about losing all sense of direction in life, especially if we are a passenger or bystander, powerless to influence events. Anxiously searching for the right road in a strange town could point to fears about losing our personal identity.

12 WEARING A MASK

The wearing of a mask in a dream relates to the appearance we present not only to others but also to ourselves. We often cannot remove the mask or are forced by others to keep it on. This may be a warning that we risk losing all contact with our true self.

SEE ALSO
12: **Pair of masks** p.80

13 VEIL

Wearing a veil over the head indicates the dreamer's wish to become invisible, according to Jungian symbolism – an introverted desire to withdraw from the outside world.

14 STRANGE REFLECTIONS IN THE MIRROR

Things seen in a dream-mirror are often said to be reflections of personal identity problems – our own face with closed eyes suggests a refusal to confront reality, while somebody else's face may indicate love or envy of that person or the dreamer's own sense of inadequacy when measured against them. No face at all may be the ultimate identity crisis: a fear of death and the annihilation of the self.

15 RAFT

A rudderless, drifting raft is a cause of alarm for some, raising fears of directionlessness and lack of control over our lives. On the other hand, as Rabbi Nachman of Bratslav (1772–1810) said, not knowing where we are going can sometimes be the best way of discovering the real self.

A raft is also a means of survival and in this sense the image can be a wholly positive one – a realization that we can ride out our sea of troubles rather than be overwhelmed.

SUCCESS AND FAILURE

16 FAME

Dreams of sudden glory and celebrity amid the applause of friends, family and strangers suggest a great need for a boost in self-esteem. On the other hand, they can also point to an ambitious readiness to undertake new challenges.

17 PRIZES

Winning the lottery or a prize can denote a general feeling of well-being, but may indicate worries about money problems. Gaining a prize may be associated with winning a loved one's sexual favours, often symbolized by a **garland of flowers (18)**.

Prizes may also warn us against unwarranted expectations. Jung cites as a universal dream-type the Greek myth of Bellerophon, who received the winged horse Pegasus from the goddess Athene, and then presumptuously tried to fly to the heavens – the god Zeus sent a gadfly to sting the horse and Bellerophon came crashing to the ground.

19 COMMUNICATION BREAKDOWN

A vain struggle to attract the attention of a loved one, a senior colleague or even someone famous whom we admire, may betray our feelings of inadequacy – or our deep frustration that the important people in our lives do not properly appreciate our real qualities.

20 RACING

Winning a race points to an underlying confidence that our true potential will be recognized; but an overzealous desire to win may reveal an exaggerated need for others to acknowledge that potential.

On the other hand, losing a race, especially if we end up being pipped at the post, indicates the frustration, even humiliation, of understanding the limits of our potential.

ANXIETY

21 FALLING

A dream of falling down a flight of stairs, from a tall building or over a cliff, may arise from anxieties that we may be overreaching our abilities in our personal or professional lives.

The fall frequently forms the climax of a dream in which we are being chased by hostile pursuers. If this is the case, falling – or jumping – is a desperate escape mechanism, but if we turn at the last minute to face our pursuers we may, after all, have the strength to confront them.

22 DROWNING

Drowning in deep water suggests floundering in the depths of the unconscious. As with dreams of pursuit, we may experience uncomfortable thoughts and feelings that we are not yet ready to bring to the surface. In extreme cases the feeling of being unable to get back to the surface may indicate the dreamer's fear of the onset of mental illness. At the very least the dream alerts us that some areas of our unconscious need to be examined, with care.

23 NARROW SPACES

Although being confined in a small space may seem to have negative implications, such a dream may in fact be a constructive inner protest, pointing to the struggle of creative energies to find expression. We may be anxious that something or someone – a tedious job or a tyrannical boss – is keeping a tight lid on our energies.

Crawling through an apparently endless narrow **tunnel (24)** is a common claustrophobic dream of

SEE ALSO
21: **Being chased** p.29

birth-anxiety. A prospective parent could experience this in identification with the coming baby; otherwise we may just be harking back to our own birth, perhaps when we are anxious about a challenging imminent event.

25 TRYING TO RUN

Impelled to flee a painful situation, dream-runners cannot move because their feet are weighted down or stuck in the mud. The brain may induce such dreams precisely to stop us acting out anxious impulses in our sleep by running in the bed – or running amok in the bedroom.

26 BEING CHASED

In cases of extreme anxiety, a dream in which we are being chased could point to feelings of paranoia or persecution that may be pushing us toward the edge; more generally such a dream may stand for certain unpalatable aspects of our personality which are usually repressed but demand to be dealt with.

27 PUSHING AGAINST THE CROWD

Dreams of vainly trying to push through the crowds in a busy bar, or in a department store at sale time, hint at barriers between the conscious and unconscious minds. Oppressive crowds between us and our goal indicate that we are inhibited in our waking life from satisfying our keenest unconscious desires.

28 SOCIAL INEPTITUDE

Forgetting our words when giving a speech before an audience, tripping up in public, treading on our partner's toes on the dance floor, or spilling a drink over a friend or a VIP can betray a deep-seated sense of social inadequacy, even among the people closest to us. On the other hand, it is worth examining the dream closely to see if such seeming ineptitude in fact contains an element of defiance – expressing our feelings of frustration with the stiflingly oppressive bonds of social convention.

29 INTIMATE STRANGERS

Meeting a close friend or lover but treating them as a total stranger can lay bare a disturbing ambivalence toward someone whom we thought we knew intimately – perhaps, in truth, we do not wish to invest all our love or trust in them.

A similar sense can be conveyed by looking on as a **spy (30)** while a close friend or lover engages in an illicit or compromising act, such as robbing a house or committing adultery.

31 FEAR OF THE UNSEEN

Not knowing who or what is out there in the darkness is perhaps the most universal of all anxiety dreams. It is experienced particularly frequently among people embarking on a course of psychoanalysis or any other therapy that will reveal hitherto unexamined areas of the self. Like conscious terror of the dark, such dreams may be rooted in ancient fears acquired when our primordial ancestors were prey to large, nocturnal carnivores.

32 WANDERING ALONE

A feeling that the source of all our problems lies outside ourselves may prompt dreams of wandering happily alone in a vast desert or dense forest, fleeing the company of others.

WELL-BEING AND OPTIMISM

33 HONEY

The sweetness of honey has long been identified with visions of happiness and well-being: in classical myth honey was the food of the gods and the biblical image of the Promised Land flowing with milk and honey is also deeply imprinted on Western culture.

34 BEES

Since ancient times bees have symbolized the virtue of industry and the prosperity that is its reward. Their appearance points to the wisdom of sticking at a project in order to attain a worthwhile goal – and, like the bee with its sting, acting to fend off those whose influence is hindering our progress.

35 GATES

A dream featuring a gateway usually suggests that our circumstances are inviting us to move forward into a new world of opportunity and insights. However, no dream symbol is without ambiguity, and gates may occasionally lead not to heaven but to hell: we would be wise to reflect carefully before embarking upon any radical new path to personal fulfilment.

36 GARDEN OF EDEN

Like the land of milk and honey, the Garden of Eden is an ancient mythic landscape of bliss and contentment – but as a paradise lost it may also warn us against complacency. Yet even if we imagine ourselves to be driven from the garden, like Adam and Eve, the vast unexplored landscape beyond can present us with an exciting new vista of challenge and opportunity.

37 LIGHT

Jung claimed that light appearing in a dream "always refers to consciousness". In this view, light is a sign that new insights are illuminating our conscious mind. Christians may link this to Jesus as "the light of the world"; and to Buddhists it may suggest the concept of the "boundless light" as the source of all creation, embodied by the *buddha* Amitabha.

38 GOOD LUCK CHARMS

The appearance of a good luck charm in a dream encourages us to have greater confidence of our success, perhaps at work or in our love life. The charm may be a personal talisman like a precious stone, a number or favourite colour, or an ancient and widely known symbol of good fortune, like an **olive branch (39)**, a **four-leafed clover (40)**, a **white dove (41)** or a **black cat (42)** – however, the latter is a symbol of death for Muslims and is considered unlucky.

43 BRIGHT COLOURS

Dreamers suddenly bathing in a blaze of bright colours may be on the cusp of an exciting new perception. For Jungians, the colours act as a prelude to a "grand dream" of archetypal themes springing from what Jung called the "collective unconscious".

SEE ALSO

38: **Jewels** p.83,

NUMBERS
pp.332–337;

43: **COLOURS**
pp.341–343

AUTHORITY AND RESPONSIBILITY

44 AND 45 RULERS

A **royal figure (44)** often relates to parental authority. In Freudian terms, dreams of dining or even having sexual relations with royalty represent classic wish-fulfilment, disclosing a deep-seated desire for intimacy that substitutes royalty for the mother or father – the supreme authority figure.

A **head of state or head of government (45)**, such as a president or prime minister, can appear as a friend seeking advice, expressing the dreamer's yearning for a closer, more confidential relationship with a parent or other important authority figure, or a desire to be entrusted with a position of responsibility.

46 BUREAUCRACY

Unlike the clear-cut authority of a police officer, our boss or our parents, bureaucracy hounds us in our dreams with its more insidious form of control. Endless corridors, identical desks and faceless functionaries can symbolize the anxieties of debt, unemployment and the oppressive anonymity of the big city. **Stacks of paper (47)** are the bureaucrat's dream – or nightmare. Ever-growing piles issue a warning to find new ways of dealing with the stress of our responsibilities.

48 PARLIAMENTS

Seats of government, such as London's Houses of Parliament or Washington's Capitol, may represent a desire to wield power over our colleagues, friends or partner. **Unruly or chaotic scenes (49)** in the debating chamber may indicate a crisis in our personal authority at work, or confusion about which of several options to follow when contemplating a course of action.

50 TALL HAT

Wearing a tall hat (such as an aristocratic black silk top hat or an English policeman's helmet) or, even more obviously, a **crown (51)**, points to feelings of superiority. Holding on to such headgear in a gale or having it knocked off in a crowd could express anxieties about status, perhaps following a promotion at work: do I deserve my more exalted position and how firm is my hold on authority?

52 TAKING CONTROL

> SEE ALSO
> 50: **Changing hats** p.78; 54: **Law court** p.232

An aspiration to exercise responsibility, or a feeling that our leadership qualities are not appreciated as they should be, can come to the fore when we dream of taking control in the midst of catastrophe, such as a fire in a theatre or panic on a sinking ship.

53 JUDGE

In Jungian terms, the judge can represent the archetype of the Wise Old Man (see p.15), who points to the dreamer's potential progress toward higher states of consciousness. If we are the judge, this suggests an appreciation of our own wisdom and powers of judgment – perhaps we should follow our "gut feelings" in some matter that preoccupies us.

On the contrary, standing before the judge as a **defendant in court (54)**, not knowing why we are there, we may be feeling persecuted by the arbitrary forces of authority. The oppressive nature of authority was a recurring theme in the dreams and fiction of the Czech writer Franz Kafka, expressed most powerfully in his novel *The Trial*.

55 PAINFUL CHOICES

Being obliged to choose one person or thing among several can allude to the dreamer's anxiety about a painful test of personal responsibility – whom to fire, whom to retain, perhaps whether to end a marriage or relationship. According to recent studies, the occurrence of such dreams has increased in response to the popularity of television game shows where contestants have to choose the weakest or least popular player, who is then expelled from the game.

Freud placed the theme of choices in the realm of the libido, where the dream expresses a latent uncertainty over one's sexual orientation.

RELATIONSHIPS

56 UNSUITABLE PARTNER

An inappropriate pairing of two objects (say, a motorbike and a bath-tub, to take an extreme example at random) might reflect a concern you have about an unsuitable partner for a son or daughter, or someone else who is close to you – or for yourself.

57 WRONG PHONE NUMBER

Repeatedly getting the wrong person on the telephone or, in its modern variation, seeing an **e-mail error message (58)** on your computer screen, may indicate a disturbing inability to communicate with someone important in your life or a loss of intimacy with a partner.

Freudians might be tempted to see phallic symbolism if you are calling on a cellphone, pointing to sex as the root of the problem.

59 CARING ACTIONS

Looking after a person in distress or helping an accident victim might appear to involve unknown people, but upon closer inspection some detail will identify the dreamer, a friend or a loved one. Such dreams may reveal an affection felt for the other person or, if we are on the receiving end of the caring action, our need for that affection.

60 FAMILY QUARRELS

An argument within a family or partnership may signify something completely different from a crisis in the relationship. Because of their identification with traditional authority, a spat with parents may symbolize doubts about religious faith. Children storming out of the house may represent the loss of parental ambitions.

61 MENDING THINGS

A real-life need to resolve a relationship problem may be symbolized by dreams about repairing something, perhaps fixing a car or glueing together some broken object.

62 BIRDS

Animals possess strong symbolic qualities and frequently represent aspects of relationships. Birds take on a meaning associated with the qualities we frequently attribute to them: for example, a bird of prey, a nest-stealing cuckoo or a thieving magpie may represent the threat of adultery, while the soft-voiced nightingale and dove suggest reconciliation or the need to soothe a troubled relationship.

SEE ALSO
57: **Mobile phone/cellphone** p.50;
62: **ANIMALS** pp.314–329

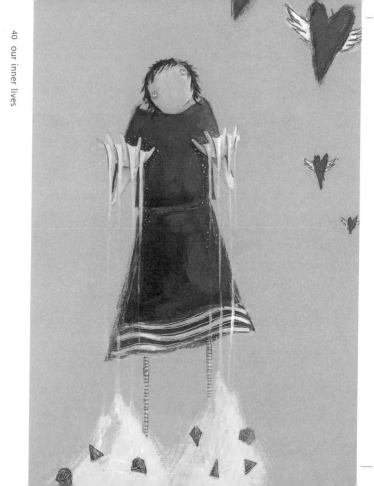

Except in their phallic form of quills, **feathers (63)** fluttering separately through the dream represent warmth and tenderness, perhaps in the sense of a peace-offering or a gesture of affection.

64 HOTELS

Hotels appear as emblems of the potentially short-lived and impermanent nature of a relationship. On the other hand, a hotel's associations with the pleasures of travelling may indicate that your emotional journey with a partner is heading toward a new level of intensity, intimacy and joy. The view from your dream-room can help clarify the meaning: it may offer a wonderful sunny vista of broad horizons – or overlook a dim and dingy alley or yard.

65 GOLD DUST RUNNING THROUGH FINGERS

Regret that an intimate relationship or cherished association is coming to an end may help to explain the dream-image of gold dust – or sometimes jewels – disappearing slowly through our fingers. A perhaps more desperate sense of love lost is conveyed by the image of running with two cupped **hands full of water (66)** to someone parched with thirst – only to see the water seep away before we reach them.

SEE ALSO

63: **Quills or pens** p.47;
64: **BUILDINGS** pp.232–248

67 FLAMES

Flames give off both heat (commonly associated with strong emotions, such as love and anger), and light (which often serves as a symbol of self-knowledge). They may reveal to us previously unseen aspects of our relationship, and in so doing guide us toward the resolution of a conflict with our partner. Bear in mind that the light that flames shed flickers and so we may have to focus hard to derive inspiration.

68 SPIDER'S WEB

The lethal web in which a spider enmeshes its prey may reflect a pro-found insecurity about intimate relationships in general, or simply a feeling that we need to extricate ourselves from a current emotional entanglement. Modern technology adds a new layer of meaning to this image of entrapment. Through a process of the sleeping mind known as "word-play analogy", keen users of the **Internet (69)** may encounter the spider's web – a warning, perhaps, about becoming trapped in an obsession with the World Wide Web.

SEE ALSO

67: **Candle** p.48,
Fire p.285;

71: **Beach**
p.153, **Country-side** p.292

70 WITCH

The Jungian archetype of the Great Mother (see p.17), a formidable, chastising figure who nurtures on the one hand and punishes and seduces on the other, may appear as an evil witch – perhaps one who seeks to devour small children, as in the fairy tale of Hansel and Gretel. For Freud, the wicked witch does not necessarily imply that we fear or hate our mother – on the contrary, it may represent repressed incestuous desire for her.

71 HARMONIOUS LANDSCAPE

A harmonious relationship may be conveyed by a serene landscape with soothing hues bathed in a gentle light. Such scenes may involve some distant childhood memory – say, with the family all together enjoying a happy day out at the beach. This may convey our nostalgia for the lost intimacy of a past relationship or for a close friendship that has drifted.

72 SILENT STARES

People staring at one another without moving or saying a word for what seems like an endless period can lay bare two quite different forms of relationship tension. The scene may bring to the surface a feeling of blocked communication – we are not getting through to someone close to us. Alternatively, the tension could be positive, indicating that now could be the right time to move a relationship forward. With bated breath, the tense and silent figures await our signal for this exciting new phase to begin.

SEXUALITY

73 EXPLOSIONS

Spectacular explosions frequently relate to orgasm. In the exhilarating form of fireworks, the orgasmic symbolism is likely to indicate a feeling of sexual well-being. More destructive explosions may express darker urges, such as the desire to dominate.

A dream of a **plane crash (74)** can of course simply express our worst fears about flying. However, analysts have noted among women patients an association between a dream of a plane crash and rape, or the fear of it. Freudian interpreters might view a man's dream of a plummeting and exploding airliner as an expression of impotence anxiety.

75 MAKING LOVE

It is not difficult to interpret a dream in which we are making love to someone to whom we are sexually attracted, especially if our desire is illicit. However, for many Jungians and other dream analysts, the act of love-making may not have a specifically sexual meaning – it may simply indicate an intense yearning for creative expression.

Freudians view a wide range of mundane activities as symbols of sexual intercourse, such as: **sliding down a banister (76)**; rhythmic **hammering or chopping (77)**; a **train entering a tunnel (78)**; and **riding a bicycle (79) or horse (80)**.

81 KISSING

Jung says that the image of kissing "derives far more from the act of nutrition than from sexuality" – the delights of dream-kissing are thus likely to be rooted in memories of suckling at our mother's breast.

82 DOMINATION

Dreams where one partner dominates the other may not overtly involve sex, but may nonetheless have sexual overtones. Casting ourselves as a dominator may mask our sexual insecurity; in the submissive role we may feel an incestuous desire for a parent. Alternatively, such dreams may stem from a strong desire to gain the upper hand in a relationship, or resentment of what we feel to be a subordinate role. The explicit eroticism of **sado-masochistic acts (83)**

SEE ALSO
78: **Tunnel**
p.27;
79: **Motorcycle**
p.129;
83: **Whips**
p.46

hints at a secret pleasure in this battle of wills; or if the relationship in question is ostensibly non-sexual – say, with a work colleague – it could indicate that a latent sexual tension is at work.

84 RED ROSE

The red rose is a traditional symbol of romantic love and erotic passion, suggesting to Freudians the female sexual organs and sometimes menstrual blood. A rose with its thorns implies an attitude toward female sexuality in general that is fraught with ambivalence – whereas the beauty of the flower is enchanting, its thorns can wound.

85 VELVET

A soft and luxurious fabric, velvet perhaps recalls the comfort of home and the generous affection of our parents, although Freudians associate velvet with pubic hair. Other analysts link velvet and **moss (86)** with a desire for the restful softness of nature, or a more general need for comfort and peace.

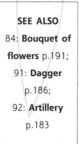

SEE ALSO
84: **Bouquet of flowers** p.191;
91: **Dagger** p.186;
92: **Artillery** p.183

87 WHIPS

Part of the classic paraphernalia of sado-masochistic sexuality, whips may symbolize a desire for – or fear of – domination, whether in the bedroom or the workplace. A similar sense may be attributed to the accompanying sado-masochistic gear of **silver chains (88)**, **leather clothing and straps (89)** and **black boots (90)**.

91 AND 92 WEAPONS

Most weapons are seen as masculine symbols, and a stabbing, swiftly penetrating **knife (91)** can represent male sexuality at its most violent, even expressing contempt for women. The reliance on a knife may lay bare a man's sexual insecurities, especially a fear of impotence, or it may represent an inner battle with dangerous desires.

Guns (92) are another image of aggressive male sexuality, with the added dimension of orgasmic symbolism in the firing of the bullet. As with a knife, wielding a gun may indicate doubts about one's virility.

93 QUILLS OR PENS

Usually held upright, quills and pens are obvious Freudian phallic symbols, especially if dipped in an inkwell. Even dream-analysts who avoid such sexual interpretations see pens as a general symbol of masculinity, linked with the power of written authority wielded by a traditionally male hierarchy. Jungians suggest that the quill or pen represents the archetype of the Animus (see p.17), the male aspect of the female psyche.

Other phallic dream-symbols include a lighted **candle (94)** and a **cigar (95)**. The candle's flame of desire may burn brightly, flicker uncertainly, or be extinguished altogether. A cigar's oral and masculine associations have been related to latent male homosexuality, although the cigar-smoking Freud discouraged overdoing such sexual symbolism with his famous comment: "Sometimes a cigar is just a cigar."

96 GUSHING WATER

Water gushing from a tap is a frequent symbol for male ejaculation, just as a cascading **waterfall (97)** may symbolize female orgasm.

SEE ALSO
94: **Flames**
p.42, **Fire**
p.285;
96: **Water**
p.284; 99:
Holy Grail
p.358; 101:
Empty purse
p.55

A bottle of **champagne (98)** spraying white foam is the most triumphant of male orgasm symbols. Such dream-orgasms – when they do not accompany the real thing – may represent our urge for creative expression.

99 CUPS

Drinking from a cup can represent oral sex with a woman. Even when identified with the Jungian image of the Holy Grail as recipient of love and truth, the cup remains an emphatically female symbol, associated with the virgin Grail-bearer or the archetype of the Great Mother (see p.17). Another mythic vessel, the **Horn of Plenty or Cornucopia (100)**, is an ambiguous sexual image: male, if it spills forth its riches and its shape is emphasized; female, if we plunge into the horn to feast on its gifts.

101 PURSES

Interpreted by Freud as a symbol of the female genitalia or womb, the purse is said to be one of the most frequent of all dream-images. A woman may be imagined offering her sexual favours when the dream-purse is open – or withholding them when it is snapped shut.

102 CHURCHES

There are few headier psychological brews than sex and religion, and the dream-church embraces both. Churches with a steeple towering above an arched portal combine both male and female symbolism

– perhaps reflecting the intimate sexual communion we feel with our partner, or simply our sense of ease with our sexuality. For a religious person, the image of a church or temple might embody any inner conflict between sexual expression and moral or religious sensibility.

103 SOCK

Socks and other items of clothing into which a part of the body fits snugly are often interpreted as representations of the female genitalia. Being put on or taken off, such items may stand for the act of intercourse. **Gloves (104)** and **shoes (105)** are other common images of this type. Shoes can also denote authority and domination – perhaps recalling times in childhood when our parents "put their foot down".

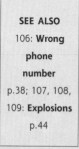

SEE ALSO
106: **Wrong phone number** p.38; 107, 108, 109: **Explosions** p.44

106 MOBILE PHONE/CELLPHONE

This modern icon of fast, sexy, have-it-now living joins the ranks of Freudian phallic dream-symbols. Taking the place of an absent loved one, the cellphone may evoke loneliness and sexual yearning or stand for the act of masturbation. A powerful tool of direct and highly personal connection, it may also figure as a malfunctioning obstacle to communication, frustrating our attempts at sexual intimacy.

ANGER AND FRUSTRATION

107, 108 AND 109 POWERFUL PHENOMENA

Images of a **bursting dam (107)**, an **erupting volcano (108)** or an **avalanche (109)** of snow or rocks may warn of an emotional explosion over-whelming our self-control – a sign that we should express some unspoken issue. More positively, the dream may also point to the release of dynamic creative energies.

110, 111, 112 AND 113 SUDDEN/VIOLENT ACTS

Unsuspected anger toward someone can be revealed by a sudden **discharge of gas or flames (110)** from a container – a bottle most vividly represents the "bottled-up" nature of such feelings. The image may take on violent proportions – **vitriol or acid (111)** thrown in some-one's face, a **photograph defaced (112)**, a **loved one decapitated (113)**. Such destructive, even hate-filled dreams indicate the urgency of dealing with our pent-up and potentially dangerous rage.

114 INABILITY TO UNDERSTAND

We are hearing a message we know to be of crucial importance, but we find ourselves unable to understand it – an experience that is even more infuriating when, as often happens, the words are clear and we know that they are in our own language. Similarly frustrating is the scenario where we are trying to explain something to someone but simply cannot make ourselves understood. Both dreams speak of an area of our lives where communication may be blocked – are we misreading the emotions of someone close to us, or being less open with them than we might?

115 FRUSTRATING TASKS

The frustrations of everyday chores at home and work may be transmuted into images of, say, trying in vain to build a house of cards, or scrubbing a vast floor with a toothbrush. Like the classical myths of the labours of Hercules (set a string of near-impossible tasks as punishment for killing his family in a fit of madness) or the torment of Sisyphus (doomed to spend eternity pushing a rock up a mountain, only to see it roll back down just before reaching the top), our infuriating or pointless dream-tasks may furnish a lesson in humility for an overweening ego.

SEE ALSO
116: **Social meals** p.150

116 BEING REFUSED A TABLE IN A RESTAURANT

Being turned away from a restaurant couples intense frustration and disappointment with a feeling of social alienation and – since eating often has an

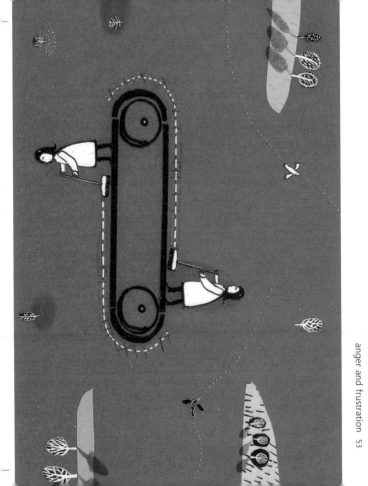

erotic dimension – perhaps also a sense of sexual inadequacy. An officious *maître d'* may stand for an overbearing parent who thwarts your personal growth, especially your sexual independence.

117 MISSING A TRAIN

Running along a platform after a departing train is a common dream-image. A train is a classic Freudian phallic symbol, suggesting a sexual cause behind frustration expressed by the dream. Or perhaps we are longing for greater intimacy with an absent or emotionally distant father. For a man, the missed train could indicate an anxiety about impotence.

Watching, or sitting in, a **stationary train (118)**, a **traffic jam (119)** or a **broken-down car (120)** may express our frustration with a relationship that seems to be lacking in direction or, worse, going nowhere. Such images, like that of vainly **trying to park a car (121)**, could also stand for an inability to identify our true place in life.

LOSS AND BEREAVEMENT

122 EMPTY PURSE

On a literal level, an empty purse might imply that we value material possessions more deeply than we realize. However, it is also a classic dream-image of bereavement, often arising from the loss of a loved one – through death, divorce or separation – and a mourning for the affection, comfort and security we derived from their presence. It may also be prompted by nostalgic memories of a never-to-be-recaptured experience, such as the carefree pleasures of childhood and youth.

123 ASHES OR DUST

Recalling the words spoken by the priest at a funeral, "ashes to ashes, dust to dust", images of ash and dust are often associated with the disappearance from our lives of a treasured person or thing. They can also symbolize laying to rest a difficult or painful emotional experience.

124 LOSING SOMEONE IN A CROWD

Commonly associated with the grieving process is the scenario of losing sight of someone we love among a great throng of people. This may be accompanied by unanticipated feelings of resentment toward our lost loved one. It is not uncommon for bereaved people to feel, in addition to the sorrow of their loss, a painful sense that the deceased has chosen to abandon them.

125 LOVED ONE RECEDING INTO THE DISTANCE

The loved one moves further and further away and eventually disappears from sight. As with the image of the deceased swallowed up in a crowd, the feelings of grief expressed by this image may be mixed with resentment at the departure of one close to us – especially if the deceased ignores our repeated attempts to attract their attention by waving or calling out to them.

On the other hand, the loved one happily **waving goodbye (126)** from a distance before they finally fade from view may indicate that our pain, too, is receding as we gradually become reconciled to the reality of our loss.

127 DARK HOUSE

A house is often interpreted as a symbol of the dreamer and represents the place where we withdraw from the outside world to live out our inner lives. A dark, cold or vacant interior can symbolize the profound sense of loss we feel when we are deprived of the warmth and light of those we love.

128 LOCKED OUT

Standing on the doorstep, unable to find the keys to our house or otherwise unable to enter, we may be experiencing great difficulties in knowing how to proceed beyond the seemingly immovable barrier of grief. Yet simply by making us aware that this barrier exists, the dream may mark the threshold of the healing process: from this point, we may be able to begin envisioning ways to ease open the doorway to a future without our departed loved one.

129 AND 130 INCONGRUOUS EMOTIONS

We are onlookers at what ought to be a cheerful or festive occasion – such as a party, a dance, a game in a stadium, a carnival – and all we can feel is intense, **inappropriate sadness (129)**. This may indicate our need to turn away from the many distractions and preoccupations with which – perhaps unconsciously – we have filled our lives in the aftermath of a great loss. These activities may have prevented us from confronting the necessity to grieve.

Conversely, we may experience **inappropriate happiness or elation (130)** in a setting which in the waking world would normally be sad, such as the death or funeral of someone dear to us. Such images may strengthen our belief in life beyond the grave, a conviction that the deceased has gone to "a better place". Alternatively, the dream could point to a state of denial – in order to protect ourselves from the searing pain of loss, we are subconsciously refusing to countenance the reality of death.

RELIGION AND SPIRITUALITY

131 HEAVEN

Heaven may appear in the traditional forms depicted in religious art – skies ablaze with light, God surrounded by angels and cherubs – and also as a familiar landscape in a beautiful, idealized form. Envisioning ourselves in this setting could symbolize our quest for spiritual or religious truth. On the other hand, standing before God enthroned also brings to mind traditional depictions of the Last Judgment – so perhaps some negative aspect of our psyche must be dealt with before we can truly enter the spiritual plane.

132 JESUS CHRIST

Jesus represents both the divine and the human. The image of Jesus on the cross appears as a multiple symbol of life, death, resurrection and salvation. Such dreams occur at critical moments of one's life – perhaps close to death or at other times when personal or spiritual issues are a major preoccupation. Jesus can also express a desire to gain personal inner peace and to serve others, as can the serenely compassionate image of the meditating **Buddha (133)**.

134 VIRGIN MARY

Embodying the ideal feminine principle in Christianity, the virgin mother of Christ symbolizes a striving for purity, compassion and grace

– perhaps indicating a sense of detachment from the sensuality and "lower" passions associated with divinities of the classical tradition such as Venus (Aphrodite), goddess of love.

135 PROPHETS AND SAINTS
Holy figures represent higher religious aspirations. These individuals may offer a stimulus to our personal quest for spiritual fulfilment.

136 ANGELS
Angels commonly take on the symbolism that Christian tradition

attributes to them, that of heavenly messengers bringing the word of God to humans. A dream of the Annunciation, when the archangel Gabriel told Mary that she would bear Christ, may occur at a time when we feel ourselves to be on the verge of spiritual transition. The archangel Michael slaying a dragon or leading the heavenly hosts against Satan is a traditional Christian symbol of light driving out the forces of darkness, perhaps pointing to a personal "demon" that our higher self needs to overcome. Angels are also identified with dead children and may fulfil a comforting role at a time of bereavement.

137 BEING OF LIGHT

Central to the Jungian interpretation of dreams, the being of light is an archetypal image embodying a universal spiritual principle. We may imagine a figure bathed in the light of the seven-branched **menorah candelabrum (138)** of Judaism, or we may picture instead the figure wearing the halo or mandorla of light that features in the imagery of a number of faiths throughout the world. Such a light may express divine energy.

139 EAGLE IN FLIGHT

The eagle soaring across the heavens is a common dream-symbol of spiritual aspirations, but its sudden fall toward the ground warns us against the dangers of taking counterproductive pride in our spiritual progress.

140 PRIEST

A priest, rabbi, pastor or other holy person may represent the authority of the Church. Such a figure may also stand for a parent dispensing spiritual and moral wisdom to us as children – perhaps we yearn for such times of simple moral certainties.

141 HINDU DEITIES

The multiple divinities of Hinduism embody a complex and powerful symbolism. Brahma is the source of the cosmos, Vishnu its protector and Shiva is the destroyer of demons and creator of life. Together with Devi, the powerful Goddess, their appearance expresses disturbing passions but also great love and creativity and liberating energies.

SEE ALSO
139: **Prizes**
p.25

THE SELF AND OTHERS

THE BODY

142 LEFT AND RIGHT SIDE

Jungians often associate dreams of the left with the unconscious and of the right with our consciousness. The left is traditionally linked with misfortune or untrustworthiness ("sinister" means "left" in Latin), and dreams focusing on the left hand or left side of the body may reflect our misgivings, perhaps unconscious, toward a person or venture. Conversely, the right is associated with good fortune and trust (someone may be our "right-hand" man or woman), and dreams of the right side may arise from a sense of well-being or optimism.

Seeing someone's **back (143)** may indicate feelings of bereavement if it is the back of a dead loved one; if the person is a living parent, perhaps we feel that they have given us insufficient support or nurturing. If it is an unidentified person or group of people the dream may reflect a more general sense of abandonment or of being "left behind" by life. If it is our own back, perhaps we are beginning to sense the approach of old age (youth is "turning its back" on us).

144 HEART

Symbolizing the emotional centre of our being, the heart expresses our need for unconditional love, nurture and emotional security. If broken or imperfectly formed, the heart may point to insecurities in your feelings toward someone close to you.

145 HAIR

Often a symbol of vanity, long hair may also express a woman's powerful sense of her own femininity. To dream of oneself with a shaven head may indicate, for both sexes, a sense of disempowerment – in the West, most people know the biblical story of Samson, whose great strength disappeared when his hair was shorn.

A **full beard (146)** represents maleness and virility, while a white beard is a sign of male wisdom and maturity – a figure so bearded perhaps represents our father. Because of their proximity to the mouth, a

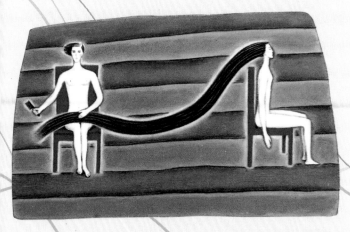

goatee beard or moustache (147) may, despite their masculine associations, refer to the female pudenda.

148 BLOOD

Blood is most frequently a symbol of life itself, but if it suddenly pours out or appears as a stain it may represent violent emotions or excessive self-sacrifice: are we exerting an effort, perhaps in a relationship, that is not truly appreciated? Blood draining away may represent the loss of life or consequent bereavement. Appearing with a female figure, the blood may be that of menstruation and in male dreamers may point to a fear of women's physicality or even to feelings of sexual aggression.

149 BONES

Bones may symbolize a desire to get to the root of a problem, to strip it to its essentials. Broken bones could point to the dreamer's perceived defects or errors, whereas a skeleton is commonly associated with death.

150 EYES

As the "windows of the soul", eyes may reflect our spiritual or psychological well-being. Shining brightly, they suggest clarity of thought, perception and purpose. Dull or closed eyes, on the other hand, may point to feelings of anxiety, emotional blockage or a lack of communication.

151 EARS

Ears may indicate a readiness to listen and respond to new insights. They may also be urging us to pay greater attention to the words and behaviour of those around us – they might be trying to tell us something.

152 FACE

We rarely see our face as others see it: in photographs the colour may not be true and in a mirror the image is reversed. Seeing our own face may therefore alert us to a need to consider who we really are and perhaps discard the face we habitually present to others. Several different faces may prompt us to focus on those who really matter in our lives.

153 HEAD

A head may symbolize an authority figure, such as our father. From the rear, it may signify an emotionally distant father, or, if he has died, a sense of loss.

154 MOUTH

For Freud, the mouth evoked the vagina and our oral fixation as an infant – our obsession with feeding at our mother's breast. In adults, the mouth may express impulsive tendencies and a desire for instant

SEE ALSO
149: **Symbols of death** p.108;
152: **Wearing a mask** p.23

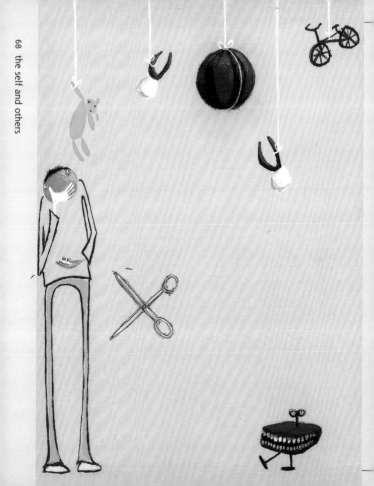

gratification. It can also represent self-expression, perhaps pointing to unspoken emotions or unexplored creativity. An open mouth may stand for the dreamer's fears of being "swallowed up" by powerful feelings.

155 TEETH
A dream of losing teeth may represent a fear of losing our youth and vitality or, by extension, our sexual powers. A broad, almost menacing display of teeth may advise a degree of caution in embracing someone who is making overtures of friendship.

156 NOSE
A prominent nose may imply the need to "follow your nose" and trust your instincts more. For Freudians, the nose is a phallic symbol. The apparently common "Pinocchio" dream of the nose growing longer as a punishment for telling lies is linked to our guilt about being less than totally honest, especially in sexual matters.

157 SKIN
The skin symbolizes the appearance we present to the world. A smooth, immaculate skin may indicate an unrealistic yearning for self-perfection. Scarred or blemished skin may express feelings of personal inadequacy.

158 HANDS

Hands symbolize action, for good or ill. Washing hands suggests a denial of responsibility, from the scene of Pontius Pilate washing his hands to indicate his innocence of Christ's death. A hand placed on a person's head is a sign of blessing, or may express a desire to dominate.

159 FINGERNAILS

Nails scratching the face of a loved one, friend or colleague are not necessarily a straight expression of hostility: they may indicate a desire to scratch below the surface and discover more about the true person.

160 ARMS

Arms may comfort and embrace, or combat and repel. Raised arms suggest authority and a threat of punishment, so are perhaps indicative of guilty feelings. Outstretched arms may express a need to protect or be protected. Arms encircling us evoke a need for consolation.

SEE ALSO
162: **Nakedness**
p.73, **Sock**
and **Shoe**
p.50

161 LEGS

Legs walking can represent an urge to move forward in a relationship or career, whereas legs running may indicate that it might be time to leave. Or is there some issue we are trying to run away from? In Freudian terms a single leg can be phallic, particularly when bared. **Feet (162)** are more specifically sexual, notably when putting on a shoe or sock.

163 BELLY

A round belly is a symbol of feminine fecundity – most obviously if it is pregnant – and may imply a wish to return to the warm shelter of the womb. In a woman, the belly may also suggest maternal feelings. The belly or abdomen is also said to represent the seat of our "gut" instincts, and feelings that cry out to be expressed.

164 BREASTS

Breasts suggest the comforts of our mother's bosom and may express our emotional insecurity or a sense of inadequate nurturing. Literally the source of life in our earliest months, breasts can symbolize for Jungians a yearning for spiritual regeneration: an unconscious desire to tap into the spiritual wellspring at the centre of our being.

165 BUTTOCKS

Large buttocks are a frequent dream-symbol of female fecundity and sexuality. Like the breasts, they may stand for our mother or, more mundanely, they may simply express frustrated sexual desire.

BIRTH AND RESURRECTION

166 FINDING AN EGG

In many mythological traditions an egg is described as the source of the cosmos and all existence. The common dream of coming across an egg is understood by Jungians to reveal that the dreamer may be ready to embark on a new phase of creativity. However, the fragility of the egg suggests that this creative energy may need to be nurtured with care.

167 DIVINE CHILD

The Divine Child is one of Jung's fundamental archetypes (see p.16), and represents regeneration, perfection and the totality of our being, as opposed to the ego, which he described as "only a bit of consciousness", floating upon "a sea of [hidden] things". Usually appearing as a child or baby, the Divine Child represents your inner spiritual potential and your power to transform yourself – perhaps issuing you with a call to pursue higher aspirations.

NUDITY AND DRESS

168 NAKEDNESS

A dream of being naked can convey quite diverse meanings. You may be yearning for a lost innocence, represented by your own naked babyhood or by Adam and Eve in the Garden of Eden. However, the naked figure may also express a latent exhibitionism – or simply a desire for sex. In the Freudian view, the **female nude (169)** is usually an expression of sexual desire for dreamers – men or women – who are sexually attracted to women. For a woman, it may point to unexplored lesbian tendencies or a desire for self-exhibition.

Freudians see the **male nude (170)** in much the same light as the female, expressing heterosexual or homosexual desire and possible exhibitionist leanings in a male dreamer. A strong and idealized figure indicates the dreamer's preoccupations with his or her father. In Jungian terms, an idealized nude of either sex might, like the naked portraits of the ancient Greek and Roman gods and goddesses, express aspirations for love or a desire to attain a higher spiritual plane.

171 NAKED CHILDREN

A naked child may be identified with the Jungian archetype of the Divine Child (see p.16) and more generally with innocence and uninhibited expression. In contrast to adults, very young children usually feel no embarrassment about being naked. Covering up a child's nudity suggests a dreamer's prudishness and perhaps a general discomfort with emotional expression.

172 ACCEPTING NUDITY OF OTHERS

Dreaming of naked people but feeling unconcerned about their nudity may suggest that, if they are people you know, you readily accept them for who they truly are; if you positively welcome their nakedness it may express a frustration with what, in waking life, you perceive to be their affected behaviour – you wish that they could be more natural.

173 OTHERS ACCEPTING YOUR NUDITY

A dream of going naked among people apparently oblivious to your nudity may suggest that you are not worried about what others think about you. It may also reveal an unconscious desire to show sides of your true personality which, in reality, you fear may not be so readily accepted by those around you.

174 DISGUST AT ANOTHER'S NUDITY

Dreamers who experience shock and outrage at the nakedness of someone they know may be expressing their unconscious anxieties about the true nature and motives of that person. On the other hand, such disgust may reveal more about yourself than the other person: your resentment

at their complete openness may be prompted by an awareness of your own inhibitions.

175 AND 176 TIGHT/LOOSE CLOTHES

If you are wearing **tight clothes (175)** you may feel constricted at work, self-conscious in public or inhibited in an intimate relationship. Tight clothes may also indicate that you are aiming at more than you can achieve in present circumstances. For Freudians, they suggest a pre-occupation with the breasts or buttocks, whose shape they reveal.

Dreamers wearing **loose clothes (176)** may be attempting to conceal their true form (and hence their true nature or identity). On the other hand, as the opposite of tight clothing, loose clothes may represent our yearning to be free of constraints and inhibitions.

177 DRESSING IN OTHER PEOPLE'S CLOTHES

Our external dress is often a symbol of our inner self. Dressing in clothes recognizably belonging to other people suggests difficulties in accepting ourselves for who we are. Apart from its obvious connotations of transvestism, for Jungians wearing clothes of the opposite sex may signal the dreamer's need to express the Anima (the female aspects of a man's nature) or the Animus (the male aspects of a woman's nature) (see p.17).

In Freudian terms, dreams of a **child dressing up in its parent's**

clothes (178), particularly if the clothes are those of the opposite-sex parent, may suggest that your childhood rivalry with one parent for the affections of your opposite-sex parent is still very much alive.

179 SHABBY CLOTHES
Dreamers dressed in shabby clothes or rags may be projecting an image of inferiority or low self-esteem. The dream may be a warning against feelings of self-pity.

180 DRESS OR SKIRT
Many women in the West habitually wear jeans or trousers nowadays, so the appearance of a dress or skirt may represent a desire, for both male and female dreamers, to express our feminine side. It could also symbolize our mother and the comforts of our early nurturing.

A **woman wearing trousers (181)** may express a desire to be – or fear of being – dominated by a woman, though this interpretation may be less valid now that trousers are no longer distinctly male attire.

182 CLOAK
The cloak may represent our tendency for concealment and secrecy, but also our yearnings for spiritual love. Freudians see in the cloak the warm embrace of female sexuality.

183 WHITE GLOVES

White gloves may symbolize a preoccupation with purity or calm. Taking them off may express a wish to have honest dealings with another person.

184 PULLOVER UNRAVELLING

The dream of a pullover or other woollen garment unravelling may indicate a growing sense of disillusionment, perhaps with cherished principles or someone we have hitherto admired. The unravelling may alert dreamers to the need to relinquish the person or ideas with which they associate the pullover and strike out in a new direction.

185 CHANGING HATS

A hat can possess a multiplicity of meanings. For Jung, a hat symbolized thought; dreamers changing hats may be at a stage of personal growth where they increasingly view long-held beliefs as "old hat", and are developing a new view of themselves and the world.

SEE ALSO
183: **Gloves**
p.50

186 TARTAN

Tartan is associated in the popular imagination with the kilt and long plaid shawl of traditional Scottish male dress, and hence may evoke images of robust virility, especially since the widely popular film *Braveheart*. For Jungians, in a woman's dream the tartan-clad Scottish Highlander might represent the archetype of the Animus (see p.17), the masculine aspects of the feminine psyche, from which the dreamer is able to draw power and vigour.

187 TURBAN

The turban is a symbol of dignity, strength and authority for the devout male Muslim or Sikh. For those outside these faiths the turban may be associated with Eastern mysticism, and hence represent the dreamer's spiritual aspirations; or it may simply stand for a sense of the exotic. In the latter case, it may point to feelings of alienation from friends, loved ones or colleagues, or a desire for more excitement in your everyday existence. By drawing attention to the head, a turban may also represent an authority figure.

188 BELT

A belt is a support, maintaining social propriety by holding up our clothes, and as such it perhaps symbolizes our anxieties about keeping up a public "face". It is also a bond, holding us tightly and restricting our freedom of movement. Loosening a belt is an ambiguous dream-image. Are we feeling guilty about something and afraid we may be caught out, "with our pants down"? Or perhaps we are feeling ready to "loosen up" and free ourselves from some of our inhibiting patterns of thought and behaviour?

189 PAIR OF MASKS

A single mask tends to represent the deceptive appearance we present to others in our waking life. A pair of masks, on the other hand, can symbolize our inherent duality – in Jungian terms, the opposed forces of light and darkness that coexist within each individual.

190 BOOTS

The boot may suggest a desire to throw off another's possessiveness or domination ("give them the boot"). Boots are what we wear to protect our feet and give us the best contact with the ground over rugged or difficult terrain, perhaps indicating that we must make a special effort to remain in touch with reality during emotionally difficult times. Changing boots can be a dream-metaphor for a recent alteration in status or a reversal of fortune – "the boot is on the other foot".

191 FUR

Freudians do not hesitate to see in fur a clear symbol of pubic hair. Dreamers who envision themselves enveloped in the comforting warmth of a fur garment may be yearning for an impossible return to the total security of life in the womb.

The immaculate whiteness of **ermine (192)** makes this fur a traditional symbol of moral purity – an attribute that accounts for its lining the robes of royalty, aristocracy, prelates and judges. Wearing white ermine in dreams may point to a longing for childhood innocence – or to delusions of grandeur.

193 UNDERCLOTHES

Underclothes can stand for feelings that we prefer to keep "under wraps". A sense of shame at being seen in public in your underwear suggests a fear of having your true opinions known.

194 ARMOUR

Being dressed like a knight points to a need to protect yourself against life's "slings and arrows". However, in donning such heavy attire you will also constrict yourself – it might be better to try to take life more easily, beginning with an attempt to be open about whatever troubles you.

195 CHAINS

Chains may appear as bonds of enslavement, indicating most obviously that we are unhappy with our commitments to our work or to a relationship. Broken chains suggest an urge to confront our feelings of discontent. A human chain may signify a hopeful link among people to further the public good.

SEE ALSO
194: **Knight**
p.85; 196:
Mouth p.67;
197–202:
COLOURS
pp.341–343

196 LIPSTICK

In Freudian terms, lipstick represents voluptuous sexuality, particularly if the dream focuses on the phallic lipstick approaching and caressing lips that represent the female genitals. If the lipstick appears to be smearing the face or body indiscriminately, the dream may express a fear of sexual violence.

197 JEWELS

Jewels may represent the qualities that we value most in ourselves or others. Thus, the unbreakable, perfect clarity of **diamonds (198)** expresses incorruptibility, integrity and the perfect wisdom of the true self. **Sapphires (199)** are the hue of the heavens and symbolize hope, joy and high aspirations; **rubies (200)** evoke the hot blood of passion and ecstasy; **emeralds (201)** are the stone of fertility and regeneration – but they are ambiguous, since green is also the shade of putrefaction.

202 PEARLS

An almost universal image of femininity, love and marriage, a pearl is a Freudian symbol of female sexuality, especially when envisioned embedded within the oyster from which it came – a symbol of the vagina – or when adorning a woman's neck as part of a pearl necklace. For Jung, pearls also express a dreamer's aspiration to purity and the transcendence of gross matter through spiritual cultivation. If the pearl is linked in the dream to someone we know, we should consider listening to the "pearl of wisdom" they have to offer.

203 TURQUOISE

In Europe and Asia, this stone is traditionally worn as protection against the "evil eye", perhaps because its exquisite blue is associated with the heavenly realm. In the Americas, too, it is linked with the heavens and the sun. In dreams it can represent our higher aspirations.

204 JADE

In Chinese myth, jade is the sperm of the Celestial Dragon, vitrified as it fell to earth. In this tradition it represents a potent union of heaven and earth, and symbolizes primal cosmic energies, fertility and the force of life. In the West, jade is more likely to bear the symbolism of its hue, green, or it may appear as a dream-wordplay: is there an aspect of your life that you feel "jaded" about and would like to change?

205 RING

For centuries a ring or band has been the symbol of matrimony. Hence, more broadly, a ring can represent commitment, fulfilment and completion. It may signal a moment of closure, perhaps an acceptance of another's loss or of the end of a relationship.

SEE ALSO
203–204:
COLOURS
pp.341–343;
205: **Wedding**
p.157, **Zero**
p.332, **Circle**
p.338; 206:
MYTH &
LEGEND
pp.354–360,
HISTORICAL
FIGURES
pp.362–367

OTHER PEOPLE

206 HERO

Displaying strength, physical perfection and courage, the hero-figure is an archetypal representation (see p.16) of our highest aspirations and striving, and may be embodied by a real or fictional person of either sex whom we greatly admire. In myth and folklore the hero often embarks on a great quest, overcoming many challenges and acquiring profound wisdom. If the dreamer is a man, Jungians would say that the fairy-tale image of a hero saving a maiden can represent an acknowledgment of the Anima, the feminine side of a man's nature. Freudians, however, would suggest that this image represents to the dreamer a domineering father-figure.

A related image is the **knight (207)** of medieval chivalry, whose valour and strength can inspire us to seek the emotional resources to meet personal challenges.

208 GIANTS

A giant might appear in a dream of childhood, when adults seemed so big to us. The giant may be an authority figure of our early years – such

as a parent, teacher or policeman – returning to threaten us with retribution for some present matter about which we feel guilty. However, giants can also be benevolent, offering reassurance and protection. Seeing yourself as a Gulliver-like giant, towering over the tiny people around you, may point to feelings of superiority, although some interpreters view this dream as a sign that we are becoming obsessed with our insecurities, blowing them out of all proportion.

209 SHADOW

The Jungian archetype of the Shadow (see p.16) represents the darker, primal aspect that is inherent in every person. The Shadow can never be eliminated, but the prejudices and other potentially destructive urges that it represents are a lifelong challenge, less likely to overwhelm us the more we are prepared to confront them.

210 BEAUTIFUL WOMAN/MAN

For a man, a young woman who embodies your idea of perfect beauty may symbolize your feminine side, the Anima, said by Jung to personify instinct, emotion and our capacity for love. Similarly, a beautiful young man may represent the Animus, the masculine side of the female psyche, personifying action, conviction and assertiveness (see p.17). Such figures encourage us to cultivate our Anima/Animus and seek strength in its qualities. The need to do so may be indicated by the way in which such images frequently disappear before the end of the dream.

211 OLD MAN

An elderly man often represents the inspirational qualities of the Wise Old Man archetype (see p.15), guiding you to personal development. However, if the figure appears senile and decrepit, the old man may express your fears of death or, especially in a man, declining sexual powers.

212 HAG

The figure of the aged hag or crone is found in folklore and myth worldwide, where she is often a woman of great longevity and wisdom. If the hag is an evil or hostile figure, in the Freudian interpretation she may represent unresolved issues in our relationship with our mother or, if the dreamer is a man, a fear of castration.

SEE ALSO
212: **Witch**
p.42; 216:
Fortune telling
p.172; 217:
MORTALITY
pp.107–109,
Black p.341

213 HOOLIGAN

The young hooligan or delinquent may be an anti-hero evoking all the negative aspects of unbridled energy. Envisioning yourself in the role of the tearaway may, in Jungian terms, be giving vent to the disturbing urges of your repressed dark side, or Shadow (see p.16). This may also express a desire to throw off inhibitions, social conventions or relationships which you feel are inhibiting creativity or personal growth.

214 BEGGAR

At the lowest end of the social scale, the beggar can remind us of the vanity of our worldly aspirations. Depending entirely on others for support, a beggar may also be a symbol of low self-esteem – or of a wish for self-abasement.

The **hobo or tramp (215)** may share the symbolism of the beggar, but can also represent a desire for freedom from the tedium and stress of everyday routines. **Gipsies (216)** are an even more evocative image of our yearning for such liberation. Their robust self-reliance, defiance of social norms and often exotic appearance add up to a powerful image for the casting off of old ways. The appearance of a fairground Gipsy fortune-teller may point to unexplored creativity.

217 WIDOW

Dressed in mourning, a widow may symbolize our apprehension of death. As one who has experienced the loss of the male energy in her life, in Freudian dream-interpretation she can be, like the hag or crone, another expression of a man's unconscious castration-fears.

218 SILENT WITNESS

Unwilling or unable to speak, the silent witness stands most obviously for some area where we are not expressing ourselves. For Jungians, stressing intellect over emotion, or vice versa, can render us metaphorically speechless, lacking the ability to communicate openly and fully with others. Until we find a better balance, true intimacy will elude us.

219 BABY

Unsurprisingly, babies frequently appear in the dreams of new parents, often in scenarios in which they are suffocated or otherwise endangered. Such dreams most likely express an obvious preoccupation with the vulnerable newcomer, but may sometimes indicate one parent's unconscious jealousy of the love being shown to the newborn.

220 TWINS

Twins may evoke opposing aspects of the dreamer's personality. If the twins are fighting, this points to a lack of acceptance of our whole self; happy twins suggest an inner harmony.

SEE ALSO
220: **Pair of masks** p.80

221 FAMILY

The appearance of your whole family can indicate that you are yearning for the comfort of childhood

and the togetherness of a home environment. On the other hand, if you see your own family but you are not present among them, perhaps you feel emotionally distant from them, even fearing the family group as a source of potential conflict.

222 MOTHER

As a dream-symbol, the mother is ambivalent. She is life-giving, a source of rebirth and continuity, but as the Mother Earth to which we return, she is a symbol of death. She represents both sexual purity and knowledge. For Freudians, she may be an object of unconscious desire, but also a figure evoking fear of castration. Jungians associate her with the Great Mother archetype (see p.17) who influences psychological growth.

Of course, a dream of your own mother may be just that: a straightforward evocation of the parent who gave us life. How she appears may point to issues in our upbringing and ongoing relationship: Are we angry or happy with her? Is she angry or happy with us? The image of the **wicked mother-in-law or stepmother (223)** may indirectly express some of these anxieties about our real mother.

224 FATHER

The dream-father plays an explicitly sexual role in the Freudian concept of the Oedipus complex (for the existence of which modern psychologists have actually found little evidence). An intimidating father may evoke a male dreamer's sexual insecurity; a loving or seductive father can reveal a female dreamer's unconscious wish for incest. For Jungians, the dream-father transcends his parental role to become a law-giver and god-like authority-figure in the manner of the Wise Old Man archetype (see p.15) – a guide, a healer, but also potentially a destroyer. Again, as with the mother, a dream of your father may simply express your current feelings toward him and issues surrounding your relationship with him.

225 BROTHER OR SISTER

Dreams of a sibling often recall childhood competition for our parents' love. The dream-death of a brother or sister may show the surprising intensity of such sibling rivalry. However, as even Freud insisted, the rivalry may just be a dream-memory and not necessarily a sign that the hostility persists in adult life.

226 UNCLE OR AUNT

Uncles and aunts are often substitutes for our father and mother. They may present more easily accepted symbols of our unconscious feelings toward our parents. For Jungians, an uncle may represent the Animus (masculine aspect) of a female dreamer, while an aunt may symbolize the Anima (feminine aspects) of a man (see p.17).

227 GRANDPARENTS

Our relationship with our grandparents is generally less fraught with the kinds of emotive issues that can characterize our attitude toward our parents, and their appearance may express a desire for just such a relatively untroubled relationship with our mother or father. For Jungians, a grandfather may symbolize the Wise Old Man (see p.15), just as a grandmother could represent the Great Mother archetype (see p.17).

228 PUBLIC MEETING

The elation we feel as we are greeted with waves of applause at a public meeting may symbolize a positive breakthrough in some difficult issue in our waking life. Perhaps someone has finally given us the approval we feel we deserve. Conversely, an anxiety dream of facing boos and catcalls may arise from a suspicion that we have not performed as well as we might, or may reflect feelings of low self-esteem, even paranoia. Such a dream may also arise from agoraphobia, a fear of facing any kind of crowd.

SEE ALSO
227: **Mother**
p.92, **Father**
p.92; 228:
Parliaments
p.36, **Making
a speech**
p.206

229 COMPANY

Dreams of hosting a group of people may express a desire to show affection to friends or family whom we feel we have neglected. Equally, however, it can express our wish to receive the affection of others. Known faces in the company may indicate who is missing from our life – a former partner or perhaps someone recently deceased.

230 CHILDREN

Dreamers who picture themselves as children may simply be recalling childhood experiences and desires. If your parents are seen showering affection on you, you may simply be missing the unconditional love you enjoyed as a child. But children can also represent aspects of your current self, such as feelings of vulnerability and innocence.

SEE ALSO
230: **Brother or sister** p.93, **Mother/Father** p.92; 232: **Intimate strangers** p.30; 233: **Rent** p.203, **House** p.237

231 NEIGHBOURS

We may project our fantasies onto the people who live in our street, whom we regularly see and greet but about whom we might know little. They may act out our latent desires, adding a welcome element of excitement to our mundane waking life.

232 FRIENDS

Friends may behave like total strangers, oblivious to our efforts to remind them that we really know each

other. Such occurrences may express our shaky self-confidence. On the other hand, the dream may suggest that we should neither expend too much energy, nor risk our integrity, in courting popularity. Perhaps it is dawning on us that we may be trying too hard to make a friendship work, because the commitment is only on one side – our own.

233 LANDLORD OR LANDLADY

A house is often interpreted as an image of the dreamer; therefore the prominent presence of someone else as the house's actual owner can represent your feelings of not being in full control of your own life. Perhaps you resent the excessive dominance of a partner or parent.

234 BOSS

A dream about your boss may simply reflect anxieties you currently have about work matters. However, your employer can also often take on many of the aspects of your father or mother. Being fired by the employer, even though there is no such threat in waking life, can recall a memory of parental rejection. Plucking up the courage to ask for a raise may bring to the surface a need for greater parental attention and love. More positively, a friendly boss can reflect a yearning for the days when someone else took responsibility for our daily welfare. If you imagine yourself as the boss, you may be expressing a desire for a dominant role in a sexual relationship.

SEE ALSO
235: **Inability**
to understand
p.51,
Intimate
strangers
p.30, **Unfamil-**
iar surround-
ings p.21

235 FOREIGNERS

A person or people speaking an unintelligible foreign language may represent a part of ourselves we do not fully understand or accept. The dream may also mirror a sense of frustrated or difficult communication with someone in our circle.

HEALTH

236 ILLNESS

A symbolic meaning may be attached to a particular dream-illness. Respiratory ailments or breathing difficulties can suggest suppressed expression or a general condition of anxiety – about work, a marriage break-up or a difficult meeting. Memories of our childhood illnesses, such as chickenpox and measles, may express a simple longing for the unconditional love of a parental cuddle.

237 AND 238 SKIN DISORDERS

In the Bible, **boils (237)** were the sixth of the ten plagues visited by God on the Egyptians to force Pharaoh to free the Hebrews; for religious dreamers familiar with that story, boils may express feelings of guilt for how they feel they have behaved toward someone in their waking life.

A boil on the foot or finger or any other part of the body that may be a phallic symbol can suggest a sexual anxiety. The skin is the symbol of how we present ourselves in public and **rashes (238)** are recognized as among the most clearly psychosomatic of disorders. A skin rash can express our inability to face the world with confidence.

239 CRIPPLE

A cripple may stand for the Trickster archetype (see p.15), mocking the pretensions of the dreamer's ego. Jung sees in a crippled woman a death-symbol of the devouring mother, but offering the potential for a rebirth. For Freud, a crippled man represents a fear of male impotence.

A **limp (240)** can be a warning from the unconscious of the danger of overweening ambition, which may bring humiliation rather than success – like that brought upon the Greek hero Bellerophon who was both crippled and disgraced when his horse Pegasus hurled him to earth for his presumptuousness in trying to fly to the abode of the gods.

241 WOUNDS

Deep flesh wounds inflicted by a knife can symbolize the female genitalia. For male and female dreamers alike, this dream-image may also express a fear of sexual aggression.

242 BLINDNESS

Dream-blindness may express some barrier to spiritual enlightenment, or a reluctance to face realities. For Freud, loss of sight represents a man's fears of being castrated. In the Greek myth that inspired the concept of the Oedipus complex, Oedipus unwittingly kills his father and marries his mother; once aware of the truth, he blinds himself – an act Freud saw as symbolic of self-castration.

SEE ALSO

240: **Prizes** p.25;

241: **Knife** p.47;

242: **Eyes** p.66

243 FAINTING

For Jungians, dreams of fainting may be prompted by a vision of a divinity or by a sudden insight into the essential nature and motivation behind a personal ambition. For Freud, such dreams relate to orgasm.

244 HOSPITAL

A dream of lying in hospital may simply be prompted by fears of getting ill. It could also indicate our desire to hand over control of some aspect of our lives to someone else. **Wards (245)** with endless lines of beds may evoke our anxiety about abandonment, perhaps at a time of crisis such as bereavement, divorce or unemployment.

246 OPERATION

Undergoing a dream-operation may signal your willingness to cut out old attitudes, prejudices and modes of thought that have hindered your psychological health.

247 MEDICINE

Medicine dispensed by a doctor, an authority figure, may point to a reliance on others to prescribe solutions to you, rather than finding your own answers. Medicine prescribed in the form of a pill may suggest an idea that you find "hard to swallow".

248 INJECTION
Being jabbed by a needle can symbolize the act of making love. If the idea of inoculation or vaccination is present, you may want to protect yourself from intrusive attentions or unwanted urges. An anaesthetic suggests a desire to deaden some powerful emotional pain.

249 HEADACHES
Any nagging problem can be referred to as a "headache", and the head can stand for an authority figure, such as your father. A dream-headache therefore suggests an unresolved issue in your relationship with an individual who has played a central and influential role in your life.

250 SCARS
Scars may carry their figurative sense of hurtful memories or traumatic experiences. They can be taken as an awareness that it might be time to examine fully the roots of the continuing pain.

251 FRACTURED LIMBS
Broken bones may reveal our insecurities. A thick plaster cast wrapped around a leg, preventing movement, can suggest a reluctance to face up to problems that may be hindering our development.

SEE ALSO
249: **Head**
p.67

252 WORKING IN A HOSPITAL

Seeing yourself as a hospital nurse or doctor perhaps expresses a desire to take charge of an area of your life where you have not felt in control. Alternatively, we may want to take command of a work situation in which we feel our superiors have been less than competent.

253 WEIGHT LOSS OR GAIN

Weight loss often indicates the wasting effect on dreamers of the possessive, demanding behaviour of family or friends. Conversely, a dreamer putting on weight may show an excessive need for their approval and a childish need for instant gratification.

BODILY FUNCTIONS

254 TOILET DREAMS

Excretion and other toilet dreams are associated by Freud with what he called the "anal" phase of a child's psychological development. In the Freudian view, our parents' mishandling of toilet training may cause us, as adults, to feel shame at these natural functions and more generally emotionally inhibited, or "anally retentive" as Freud put it.

By extension, the act of excretion can symbolize artistic expression and creativity that might have been repressed, and constipation may stand for miserliness, pent-up rage or sexual frustration. Jungians regard dreams of excretion as indicating our anxiety in public or (as with Freud) a need for self-expression.

255 WASHING AND BATHING

Vigorous cleansing of the body may stand for our obsessive need to rid ourselves of something that we regard as shameful or immoral – sometimes symbolized by a stain that will not disappear. More relaxed bathing in a warm bath may express a wish to return to the comfort of the mother's womb.

SEE ALSO
255: **Water**
p.284; 256:
Waterfall p.312

256 SHOWERING

A shower has, for Jungians, connotations of an act of rejuvenation or purification prior to a new stage of life or the attainment of a new level of consciousness. A dream that focuses specifically on **washing hair (257)** may be associated with our desire to rid ourselves of a partner, friend or colleague, echoing the song from the musical comedy *South Pacific*: *"I'm gonna wash that man right out of my hair."*

258 TOWEL

Rubbing the body with a towel can be a dream-symbol of masturbation, which in turn is likely to express sexual frustration. Guilt-feelings associated with masturbation-dreams may occur if your parents handled your adolescent sexuality with awkwardness rather than sensitivity.

259 LACK OF PRIVACY

Dreaming of ourselves exposed to public view while bathing or on the lavatory can suggest our anxieties about being "found out" – a common neurosis whether or not we genuinely have anything unpleasant to hide. In Freudian terms, the dreamer may also feel frustrated at not finding a proper opportunity for greater creativity. On the other hand, dreamers openly flaunting their toilet functions may reveal anger at not receiving sufficient public approval for their creativity.

SEE ALSO
257: **Hair**
p.65; 259:
Nakedness
p.73

MORTALITY

260 FUNERAL

Dreaming of a funeral often expresses a solemn reflection not on death but on a moment of closure, such as leaving a job or moving house. A funeral for someone who is still alive can signal regret that a relationship is over or, on the other hand, a desire to end a relationship.

261 BURIAL

Burial may suggest an unconscious repression of desires or anxieties, or alternatively a welcome ending to a traumatic phase in the dreamer's life. Burying someone alive may express hostility toward them, though not necessarily a desire for their death. Being buried alive yourself can indicate real or figurative feelings of claustrophobia.

262 COFFIN

As an open container, the coffin for Freudians can be a – sombre – symbol of female sexuality. If you are lying in a coffin, it may represent your fears of death, but instead it may indicate your sense that your old life is passing away and an exciting new phase is beginning for you.

263 AND 264 GRAVE/TOMB

An open, empty **grave (263)** may beckon us to abandon present, perhaps unsatisfying pursuits and start out on a new path. Jungians might link a **monumental tomb (264)** to the Great Mother archetype (see p.17), embracing us within her bosom. The tomb then becomes a place of security, growth and rebirth, signalling a time to turn from material to spiritual preoccupations.

265 SYMBOLS OF DEATH

Often engraved on old tombstones are skulls, skeletons, the Reaper and his scythe or an hourglass. All may appear in dreams to remind us that we have an all too limited time for personal fulfilment. They can also occur when we feel under pressure to meet a strict deadline.

266 CEMETERY

Cemeteries do not necessarily play a morbid role in our dreams. They can represent family unity, that place of eventual reunions.

evoking a continuity between past and present generations, reaffirming bonds of love.

267 NEWSPAPER OBITUARY

Many dreamers have the experience of reading of their deaths in a newspaper. This dream can point to anxieties about losing your job or your popularity. Reading someone else's obituary may express a hostility hitherto unacknowledged toward that person.

268 HANGING

Being executed by hanging is a Freudian symbol of male castration-anxiety, which in turn often simply expresses a man's sexual insecurities. The **guillotine (269)** is an even more graphic castration symbol.

SEE ALSO
264: **Pyramid**
p.339; 269:
**Loved one
decapitated**
p.51

ACTIVITIES AND STATES OF BEING

CAPTIVITY AND FREEDOM

270 AND 271 CONFINEMENT

A **prison (270)** can often stand for a set of beliefs and behaviour patterns that inhibit the dreamer's personal development. These may derive from the restrictive modes of thought we have inherited from strict or authoritarian, or perhaps just fearful, parents. The dream may take us one step toward our escape from the mental prison of such thought-patterns, by leading us to examine the circumstances that trigger them.

A similar symbol of psychological entrapment, a **cage (271)** may represent our frustration with our home, marriage or job. Dreaming of ourselves caged in the middle of a crowd may express feelings of inferiority, or our desire to break with social conventions.

SEE ALSO

270: **Breaking out of jail** p.115; 272: **Domination** p.45; **Sado-masochistic acts** p.45, **Whips** p.46

272 BEING TIED UP OR SHACKLED

The person you see being bound may be someone over whom you seek sexual or professional domination. Or, if the captive is yourself, you may be harking back to a childhood with domineering parents or feeling resentment toward an oppressive authority figure. Freud believed that there may also be an element of repressed sexual fantasies to such dreams – a desire to indulge in some form of bondage or sado-masochistic sex.

273 AND 274 LIBERATION
Breaking free from bonds or shackles (273) points to a desire for a release from a situation, such as a relationship, which is placing you under stress. If you are religious, perhaps you are finding the spiritual or even physical demands of your faith difficult: it might be time to develop a less stringent form of devotion. **Freeing animals (274)** may express the need specifically to liberate creative energies.

275 LOCK AND KEY

A lock is commonly interpreted as a symbol for the female sexual organs, with the corresponding key representing a phallus. A dream of unlocking a box may evoke sexuality as a liberating experience. If the box will not open, dreamers may feel sexually frustrated, if they are single; or, if they have a partner, they may be dissatisfied by the sexual side of the relationship.

276 TRAP

Animals often represent our unconstrained creative or destructive energies. A lethal trap to catch mice or other relatively harmless animals may suggest that you feel your creative powers to be stifled. The dream may be a call to examine what is constraining these powers and what changes you will need to effect in order to give them free rein. This could involve a change of environment or career or, less radically, simply seeking ways to schedule more time for creativity.

277 LEAVING JAIL

The elation surrounding a dream of leaving jail may reflect our positive feelings about a new phase of opportunity in our life – perhaps following our recovery from debilitating illness or the recognition of our efforts at work. However, if no such joy accompanies liberation, the dream may evoke an anxiety about being unequal to the challenges of total freedom.

Breaking out of jail (278), sometimes shown by climbing a high wall, frequently testifies to a determination to create your own chances and give free rein to emotional urges or creative talents that have too long been held in check. However, according to some interpreters, such dreams may bear the darker symbolism of a yearning for the ultimate release – to escape from life itself. If you have been feeling low or depressed, this could signal the moment to consider seeking serious, professional help.

279 KIDNAPPING

A kidnapping can most obviously express a desire to dominate or be dominated by another person, depending on whether you appear as captor or captive. Such images may contain a dream-version of the so-called "Stockholm syndrome", whereby victims end up sympathizing with their captors. If you are the victim yet find the experience surprisingly unterrifying or even pleasant, this perhaps lends a sexual connotation to the dream – especially if your captor is someone you know.

SEE ALSO
277: **Confinement** p.112;
278: **Domination** p.45; 279: **Being chased** p.29; **Breaking free from bonds or shackles** p.113

ASCENDING AND DESCENDING

280 STEPS AND STAIRS

With its rhythmic motion, going up and down steps or stairs presents a Freudian symbol of intercourse. A long, straight staircase is sometimes a phallic symbol, just as the stairwell may symbolize the female genitalia. More modern interpretations may view climbing stairs as an expression of personal growth and developing emotional maturity. Descending or falling down stairs may express anxiety about "climbing too high" in some aspect of your life – that is, overestimating your abilities.

Related to the staircase is the **ladder (281)**, a Jungian archetype for the link between the spiritual and physical life, expressed for Jung in the biblical story of Jacob's dream of angels ascending and descending a ladder or stairway between heaven and earth. Climbing a ladder can also share the same sexual connotations as stairs.

282 ELEVATOR

The elevator or lift and its shaft share the sexual symbolism of the train and tunnel. The effortless ride in an elevator at the mere push of a button may evoke the sensation, exhilarating or frightening, of being a totally passive sexual partner. In Jungian terms, the elevator represents the interplay between the conscious and the unconscious.

283 CLIMBING A MOUNTAIN

A mountain, hill or cliff may represent a current obstacle or difficulty, and climbing represents the strenuous task we have of overcoming it. For Freud, mountains and hills resemble breasts and a yearning for the maternal embrace. Jungians see mountains as the elevated spiritual plane to which we may aspire; climbing expresses the effort needed to reach those heights.

> **SEE ALSO**
> 280: **Falling**
> p.26; 282: **Train**
> **entering**
> **a tunnel** p.45

284 VERTIGO

Vertigo, the dizzy, confused sensation experienced when looking down from a great height, may express anxiety about the ever greater demands being made on you at home or work. The dream may be prompting you to be realistic and honest in acknowledging your stress, both to yourself and to those – such as your partner or boss – who may be in a position to offer relief.

285 TRIPPING OR STUMBLING

An accidental trip may be a metaphor for social awkwardness – perhaps you are anxious about "getting off on the wrong foot" with new acquaintances or important colleagues. It might also be a symptom that your self-esteem needs a boost. Stumbling may also indicate that you are spending too much time in your head, over-relying on your ability to intellectualize emotional and psychological issues.

SEE ALSO
288: **Falling** p.26, **Hang glider** p.120, **Hot air balloons** p.120, **Prizes** p.25

286 SLIPPERY SLOPE

Trying in vain to climb a muddy slope suggests that you may have taken on more than you can comfortably cope with – you may be in peril of backsliding under the pressure. This could also be a warning against becoming a "control freak": you cannot control everything and may need to show more regard to the views of others when making plans.

FLYING AND HOVERING

287 FLYING UNAIDED

Dreams of flying through the air may convey a sensation of ease and elation. Wholly detached from preoccupations of the material world, dreamers may feel on an exalted spiritual plane, at one with the universe. Some people reporting such dreams claim to have felt a sense of being in touch with their own immortality. Flying may also point to a need to get your emotional bearings by taking an overview of the many aspects of your life.

288 HOVERING IN THE SKY

Hovering or floating in the sky, looking down on the Earth below, may represent current feelings of optimism and success – the world is at your feet. But the dream depicts an impossibility and may be a warning from the unconscious against overweening ambition, perhaps stemming from a secretly held recognition that you have been trying to achieve too much too fast in your social or professional life – "how are the mighty fallen," as the saying goes. The dream alerts you to the possibility of being brought "down to earth with a bump".

289 PARACHUTE

A parachute opening as we fall may express our relief following a dangerous event such as an operation or a car accident. Offering a safe way of falling rather than a means to fly, a parachute may be a prompt from the unconscious that we should perhaps seek for early opportunities to "bale out" with dignity from some activity or emotional entanglement where, if we are being honest, we perhaps feel less than completely comfortable.

290 AIRCRAFT

Aircraft represent the desire to travel or simply to do something more exciting. In the Freudian tradition, an airplane joins the list of phallic symbols, often associated with a new sexual adventure.

Dreams of being aboard a **hijacked plane (291)** may express, most obviously, anxieties about flying; but they may also represent a fear of sexual violation or rape, particularly in women.

SEE ALSO
291: **Plane crash** p.44;
292: **Hovering in the sky** p.119; 293:
Flying unaided p.119

Hot air balloons (292) are a common fantasy-symbol expressing a desire to soar above humdrum worldly cares. You could be seeking a new perspective on your life, your enthusiasm and drive represented by the fire heating the hot air – something to be watched carefully in case it falters or goes out and jeopardizes the whole venture.

Flying in a **hang glider (293)** may share the exhilaration of flying unaided, but with a significant

difference: the hang glider may be pictured being launched from a mountain or cliff, a Freudian symbol of the sexual act – which would explain the subsequent exhilaration.

294 FLYING IN AN INCONGRUOUS VEHICLE

If we envision ourselves flying in, say, a bed or an armchair, we may wish for adventures that are not too radical a break from present routines and creature comforts. Flying on a bicycle may recall what is by now the almost folkloric image of Steven Spielberg's friendly alien in the movie *E.T.*, bicycling back to his planet – suggesting our own nostalgic yearning for home.

295 FLYING A KITE

The kite can symbolize a heady sense of freedom, perhaps at a time when the dreamer is leaving behind old pressures or embarking on an exciting new phase in his or her life. As with kite-flying, liberation is best enjoyed if we also keep our feet firmly on the

ground and one eye on the practical side of life. The
kite could also represent an ambitious but risky plan in
which you are currently involved being buffeted
by uncertainties.

TRAVEL
AND MOTION

296 GOING ON A JOURNEY

Associated in part with the rhythm of imagined motion, dreams of
going on a journey represent in the Freudian view a wish for sexual
intercourse. For Jung, travelling carries a sense of progress toward your
professional or spiritual destination. A modern
approach might see in such dreams a desire for
change in some aspect of your life, a desire to
"move on".

According to Jung, **journeying toward the
west (297)** – following the setting sun – may
suggest a sense of the approach of old age or death.
Journeying east (298), on the other hand,
indicates rejuvenation.

SEE ALSO
294:
Absurdities
p.350;
296: **Path**
p.133, **Road**
p.133

299 DEPARTURE

Setting off on a journey may suggest the dreamer is setting out on a quest for the meaning to their existence. Another common death-dream is associated with **packed bags (300)**. Being unwilling to let go of baggage suggests a desire to ward off death. Conversely, baggage left on the platform suggests a willingness to let go of life's trappings and a readiness to enter a new phase of existence.

301 RAIL TRAVEL

An interpretation of train journeys might focus on the fixed route of the rails. As with travelling on a **tram (302)**, we may feel that we are no longer controlling our own destiny and have grown too dependent on somebody else. The regular pumping and puffing of an old steam locomotive is another Freudian symbol of sexual intercourse; similarly, a train entering a tunnel. A **broken-down or derailed train (303)** can be a blessing in disguise. What at first looks like an image of disrupted plans and hopes may perhaps be telling you that you should not take the train at all – in other words, that you should not necessarily follow a certain course you had mapped out for yourself. Instead, you might head for the open road and enjoy the freedom of tracing your own route to self-fulfilment.

304 AIRPORT

As a point of departure, an airport may play a symbolic role in dreams of spiritual questing. Noisy and crowded, it may evoke the stress of a past phase that you are happy to leave behind. However, looking in vain for a familiar face to see you off may suggest that there are a few things about the old life that you will miss after all.

305 CAR JOURNEY

Freud regarded a smooth car journey as indicative of the patient's satisfaction with steady progress in psychoanalysis. By the same token, a bumpy road indicates a difficulty in accepting less palatable revelations about the unconscious mind.

Taking a **taxi (306)** can symbolize a tendency to take a back seat in life and let others do the driving, rather than relying on your own efforts. However, if you see yourself driving the taxi, the image may express a willingness to guide others on their personal journey.

SEE ALSO
299: **Loved one receding** p.56;
301: **Train entering a tunnel** p.45;
303: **Stationary train** p.54;
304: **Aircraft** p.120; 305: **Car losing control** p.23

307 SEA VOYAGE

For Jungians, a sea voyage is an exploration of the deep waters of the unconscious. This interpretation is epitomized in the archetypal image of Jonah's biblical voyage, which ended in the belly of the whale: Jonah was released only when he accepted his mission from God, which Jungians might see as embracing the messages of our unconscious rather than fleeing from them. Because Freudians consider the sea as a primary symbol of the mother and more specifically the womb, a sea voyage may also express an incest-wish.

308 SHIP

Freudians see a ship as a phallic symbol – the size of the ship indicating the degree of preoccupation with sexual intercourse. A ship tossed about in rough seas may point to a turbulent phase in the dreamer's sexuality. A **sinking ship (309)** may symbolize a doomed love.

A **ferry (310)** is the archetypal vessel associated with transitions from one state of consciousness to another, whereby we arrive at a perhaps more acute vision of personal truth. The ferryman, who must be paid for rendering his services, may symbolize the archetypal Wise Old Man (see p.15) guiding the dreamer and commanding his or her attention.

SEE ALSO
307: **Whale**
p.328

311 DOCKS

Docks may be a welcome haven, a reassuring respite after a difficult period in our life. However, as travel-dreams more often picture departures and the journey itself (our past and our present) than arrivals and journey's end (our uncertain future), docks may evoke the safe ground being left behind as we begin our voyage across uncharted seas of self-discovery. It would be usual for such dreams to be tinged with anxiety.

312 RIVER CROSSING

In Greek mythology, five rivers (known as Acheron, Styx, Cocytus, Lethe and Phlegethon) were said to link the realm of the living with the land of the dead (the underworld). As a result, dreams of river crossings are often associated with death (travelling from this life to the next) – or a journey into the dark regions of the unconscious.

313 ROWBOAT OR CANOE

The physical effort of rowing a boat or paddling a canoe may be emphasizing the demands of your personal voyage to explore your

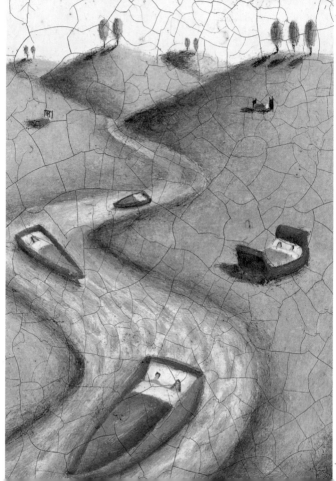

unconscious. For Freudians, the vessel may be a phallic symbol – in which case the acts of rowing or paddling suggest masturbation.

314 HORSE-DRAWN VEHICLE

The old-fashioned image of a horse and carriage or cart may suggest that you prefer to plod on through life laden with your old emotional baggage rather than seeking to advance your personal development by submitting to modern approaches, such as psychoanalysis. However, such vehicles often appear with the horses galloping out of control, signalling our inability to control our own destiny.

315 BUS

According to the Jungian view, riding on a bus, or on any other form of public transportation, suggests that the dreamer is being too conformist. Therefore, a bus dream can alert us to becoming more independent in our thinking.

316 MOTORCYCLE

A motorbike can be a strong and often exhilarating symbol of personal autonomy. In the Jungian view, anyone who dreams of riding a motorcycle is determined to be in control of his or her own destiny.

SEE ALSO
316: **Riding a bicycle** p.45

Like a bicycle, the twin-wheeled motorcycle also symbolizes the balance necessary to make progress, between conscious aspirations and the deeper impulses of the unconscious. A focus on the speed of the motorcycle places an even stronger emphasis on desire for independence.

In the Freudian view, the sexual symbolism of straddling a bicycle is asserted even more powerfully in the case of a motorcycle.

317 WHEEL

The prominence of a wheel may be a dynamic call to action. To Jungians, the wheel symbolizes the sun, representing the libido as a psychic life-force. Jung saw in the wheel's spokes a powerful phallic symbol but regarded this sexuality as an expression of an individual's total creative energies. For Buddhists and Hindus, a spoked wheel represents universal truth and justice (embodied for Buddhists in the teachings of the Buddha).

SEE ALSO
317: **The Buddha** p.58, **Circle** p.338, **Ring** p.84, **Zero** p.332

318 CROSSROADS

Crossroads are a potent dream-image signalling a time to make important choices – a new partner or job, or a new philosophical approach in life. Choices made at crossroads also entail rejections, and the dream may picture surprise features on the road the

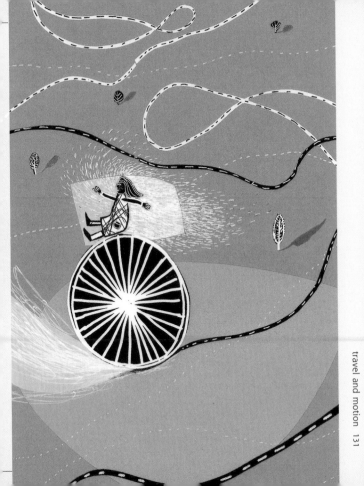

dreamer is not taking: a friend left behind, or perhaps an abandoned church symbolizing disillusionment with religious faith.

319 BUSTLE OR CONGESTION

Bustling crowds or encountering congestion in a dream may represent frustration or feelings of being obstructed in your progress toward a certain goal. If you live in a city, your dream may reveal feelings of oppression brought on by a stressful urban existence.

SEE ALSO

320: **Forest or wood** p.294;

321: **Legs** p.70;

322: **Climbing a mountain** p.117; 323: **Broken-down or derailed train** p.124, **Crossroads** p.130, **Bridge** p.21

320 WALKING

People who dream of walking may be seeing themselves in philosophical mood, as the walking figure is a classical symbol of the solitary thinker. The surrounding landscape may give clues as to the issues concerning the dreamer.

321 RUNNING

Running may express impatience to reach a conclusion. Running-dreams can also symbolize an attitude to society in general, or a desire to please others or to flee their company, depending on whether you are running toward or away from other people.

322 PATH

A path suggests that you are considering your direction in life. A rocky path can
suggest obstacles on the way to self-awareness or fulfilment. If the path
suddenly turns steeply uphill, a Freudian view might see the climb as
representing a desire for sexual intercourse.

323 ROAD

The open road is a frequent symbol of freedom. A narrow
road may emphasize the journey's moral constraints. Dreams of travelling along a
major highway can express the
dreamer's desire to fast-track to
greater self-awareness, or spiritual
enlightenment – especially if the
highway is elevated. A fork in the
road can reflect our difficulties in
reaching an important decision.

324 TOWPATH

A dream-image of a towpath alongside a canal or other waterway may feature a horse or even a dreamer towing a barge. The towpath suggests you feel that your life's journey is being slowed by the heavy burden of troublesome emotions symbolized by the barge – which is itself perhaps a symbol of male sexuality.

325 DUST

Shaking the dust from your shoes can symbolize a break with the past – whether it be in the sphere of home, work, family or friends. Dust is a symbol of the earth from which, according to Jewish and Christian tradition, we were created and to which we all return. Gathering dust on the road may echo our ponderings of mortality and encroaching age.

SEE ALSO
326: **Horse
race** p.174;
327: **Drowning**
p.27, **The sea**
p.284, **Water**
p.284

326 RIDING

Viewed as a pleasant and calming activity, horse-riding harks back to a slower pace of life, more in tune with the rhythms of nature, and so may express our desire to take life a bit easier. However, riding at a furious gallop points to a competitive streak in your personality, especially if dreaming of yourself in a race. Falling from the horse or being thrown by it points to a fear that we may have taken on some task or person in our life that we are finding difficult to cope with.

For Freud, the straddling of a horse and the rhythmic movement of the ride make equestrian dreams an unequivocal expression of sexual intercourse. The gallop may express passionate, erotic excitement, just as a trot evokes more gentle sexual enjoyment of sex.

327 SWIMMING

Swimming is often interpreted as a symbol of birth, expressing a wish to return to the waters of the womb. For Jung, a dream that involves swimming toward land is suggestive of rebirth. Swimming against the tide could mean some personal struggle. If the dreamer is swimming in the sea (a powerful, male symbol), the dream may have sexual connotations.

EATING AND FOOD

328 EATING

Since before the time of Freud, dreams of eating have been associated with sexuality. Cultures all over the world have expressed in sexual terms the pleasures of eating certain fruit, vegetables and fish. Freud attributes this sexuality to children's discovery of the mouth as the first "erogenous zone". Children express their developing sexual appetite in their eagerness to eat anything they can lay their hands on. In dreams, a similar adult voraciousness can be linked to a desire for sexual gratification.

329 MEAT

In hunter–gatherer societies meat ·has symbolized the energy, strength and other qualities of the dead animal or enemy. In modern dreamers, meat-eating may symbolize your overtly sexual side – any repressed uncon-

scious urges to partake of carnal activities – the
pleasures of the "flesh".

330 INNARDS OR OFFAL

Often discarded rather than eaten, the intestines
and guts of an animal may figure as an expression of deep urges
considered repellent by your conscious mind. The context in which
they appear may reflect your "gut" feelings about ideas currently set
before you.

331 HAM OR BACON

Conjuring up for many a nostalgic memory of homely family meals,
ham and bacon can be powerful symbols of a desire for the simple comforts of childhood. For Jews and Muslims, however, these are prohibited
foods, and in consequence might express a very different sense of not
belonging; or, alternatively, displeasure or disgust. They might also

express perhaps an urge to rebel or to explore beyond cultural conventions.

As a colloquialism meaning thigh, "ham" might also indicate a desire for sexual intercourse.

332 FISH

For Jung, a fish may refer to the unborn child, "because the child before its birth lives in water like a fish". Thus the fish may symbolize the life-force with which the dreamer is trying to make contact. Freud says that fish are a genital symbol. In this interpretation, a dream-fish has a different sexual connotation depending on whether it is opened, eaten or just looked at. **Fishing (333)** suggests probing the unconscious, but keeping our feet rooted to the ground.

Eels (334), because of their shape, are Freudian phallic symbols. Your sexual openness or otherwise may be revealed in the pleasure or disgust that these creatures inspire.

335 OYSTERS

Associated with the pearl that they sometimes conceal, oysters are invoked by

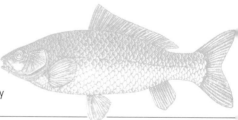

Jungians as an ancient dream-symbol of purity and humility. For Freudians, the oyster with or without its pearl symbolizes the female genitals in a vividly sensual form.

336 VEGETABLES

A common dream-image presents a variety of vegetables in great profusion suggesting our desire to enjoy the good, wholesome produce of nature. However, dreams of yearning for abundance may, in fact, reflect concerns about your lack of money or prosperity.

337 CUCUMBER

A dream-cigar may sometimes just be a cigar, as Freud put it, but he would have argued that a cucumber is rarely just a cucumber. The size of the vegetable may offer a surprising insight into the extent of your libidinous appetite.

338 FRUITS

Fruits appearing in abundance are an archetypal symbol of fertility. At a deeper level, the fruits may signify fulfilment and the rewards of creativity, or perhaps a desire to be pregnant.

SEE ALSO
332: **Swimming** p.135, **The sea** p.284; 335: **Pearls** p.83; 337: **Cigar** p.48; 338: **Horn of Plenty** p.49

339 SPAGHETTI

Spaghetti is a rich erotic symbol evoking male or female genitals or pubic hair. Dreamers may wallow in a tub of pasta or discover that their long hair has turned into spaghetti. Such dreams may express a need to satisfy the demands of the libido.

340 APPLE

From Hebrew and other ancient lore, the apple provides a rich symbolism denoting knowledge both spiritual and carnal. As the forbidden fruit through which Adam and Eve gained self-knowledge, resulting in them being turned out of paradise by God, the apple may symbolize a desire to return to lost innocence. **Stealing apples (341)** may represent a desire for an illicit sexual relationship, whether adulterous or incestuous.

A popular image of motherhood and the comforts of home, **apple pie (342)** probably conjures up a desire to return to the security of childhood. Old rivalries may be expressed if we appear to be dealt a smaller slice of pie than one of our siblings.

SEE ALSO
340: **Garden of Eden** p.32

343 GRAPES

Grapes are a quintessential symbol of sensual pleasure. They are a fruit to be shared with the loved one, placed in the other's mouth, in gentle erotic play.

Grapes therefore express sexuality in all its oral and tactile joy. In dreams, sour grapes may symbolize disgust or displeasure.

Owing its existence to grapes, **wine (344)** is the dream-symbol of a free spirit – the sense of intoxication enables us to rise above our mundane existence. Red wine may be a symbol of blood, the force of life itself; and, for Christians, it may connote specifically the blood of Christ.

345 FIGS

Figs are often seen as a female sexual symbol because of their appearance when split open to be eaten. In some societies, however, figs symbolize the testicles. In any case, this luscious fruit full of seeds is a symbol of fertility associated with our libidos. According to biblical tradition, fig-leaves were used by Adam and Eve to protect their new-found sexual modesty.

346 PEACHES

Succulent peaches most often appear as the symbol of the lasciviousness that they represent in many cultures. In Chinese tradition, though, peaches are symbols of purity and immortality.

347 BANANAS

Dreams of peeling a banana may have a considerable erotic charge, and the banana itself is an evidently phallic symbol. The banana was regarded by Buddha as a symbol of fragility. A **banana skin (348)** lying in your path on the ground might represent your misgivings about proceeding with a particular task or enterprise.

349 CORNFLAKES

Modern symbolism, often built up through marketing and advertising campaigns, links cornflakes and other popular breakfast meals with a happy, healthy and ordered home life. Dreaming of sitting at the breakfast table, especially if loved ones are present, may express a desire for improved domestic circumstances, or a move toward a life based on traditional family values.

350 OATMEAL OR PORRIDGE

These foods are associated with the nurturing comforts of our early years – as in the symbolism suggested in the nursery tale *Goldilocks and the Three Bears*. However, the image of the sticky glutinous oats could stand for emotional difficulty.

SEE ALSO

350: **Bog or swamp** p.308, **Quicksand** p.308

351 BREAD

Through its identification with wheat, the "staff of life", and hence with the nurturing Earth, bread is a traditional symbol of sexuality or fertility. The shape of the loaf can influence bread's sexual significance: round loaves may evoke pregnancy, while a French stick or baguette has an obvious connotation of male sexuality.

352 EGGS

Eggs are a universal symbol of birth and creation. According to Freud, the male dreamer may associate the image with his mother and a possible desire for incest with her. For Jung, the association is with spiritual birth or rebirth, and the emergence of new potential in one's life. A **broken egg (353)** can suggest the fragility of that potential and the need to nurture it with considerable care.

SEE ALSO
351: **The Earth** p.374; 352: **Finding an egg** p.72; 354 and 357: **Social meals** p.150

354 TOAST

For many people, toast is another great "comfort food", and as such may appear as a nostalgic symbol of home life and family togetherness. **Burnt toast (355)** can tinge the memory with anguish or melancholy about a broken home.

356 MASHED POTATO

Another comfort food, mashed potato may evoke memories of a harmonious childhood if it is a smooth and delicious concoction. Mashed potato that is lumpy and tasteless or too salty may be associated with school meals and childhood or adolescent neuroses.

357 GINGERBREAD HOUSE OR PLUM-PUDDING

The dream image of a gingerbread house or plum-pudding is inevitably associated with Christmases past. The dreamer may be yearning to recapture the warmth of childhood family celebrations.

358 JAM

The dream-symbolism of jam may not be at all sweet. Like other red substances, strawberry or raspberry jam can represent blood and may express anger, fear of violence, or sexual anxiety linked to menstruation or virginity. By dream wordplay, jam may also symbolize an awkward situation from which we are finding it difficult to extricate ourselves.

359 AND 360 FASTING AND GORGING

Freudian dream-interpretation often sees the act of eating as the satisfaction of sexual desire. **Fasting (359)** denies us that satisfaction and may represent some sex-related feelings of guilt.

Gorging (360) may stand for intense sexual lust deriving from feelings of deprivation. Eating is also a means of destruction, so gorging may express suppressed anger toward something or someone – especially if in the dream you were behaving like a wild beast, vigorously and ferociously tearing apart whatever you were devouring.

361 BUTTER

Once used in the preparation of sacrificial meats, butter symbolizes a source of sacred energy. Butter may be associated with prayer or, more generally, an urge to invoke the help of a superior force.

362 DRINKING

Liquid of any kind is often viewed as a symbol of the "life-force". Therefore, dreams of drinking may reveal a desire to understand the nature of existence. Dreams of drinking to excess (feeling inebriated or gorged on drink) may express a need to reach a higher level of consciousness.

SEE ALSO
362: **Wine**
p.142

363 AND 364 COFFEE AND TEA

Coffee (363) may indicate your wish for more stimuli in the routine of your waking life. The social aspects of coffee-drinking may indicate a need for closer contact with friends. **Tea (364)** can have a

more domesticated image and points perhaps to your longing for a break from stress or a more settled home life.

The **urn or vending machine (365)** from which tea or coffee is dispensed in an office may suggest a desire to get to know your colleagues better. It may even connote a sexual desire for one particular colleague.

366 MILK

Jungians emphasize the maternal dream-symbolism of milk, representing a mother's tenderness and nourishment, in both the physical and

psychological senses. For Freudians, milk may also have associations with the dreamer's mother, especially if the emphasis is on consuming it. However, like other white or pale-hued liquids such as **cream (367)**, milk is often said to symbolize the male's semen.

368 WEDDING CAKE

Dreamers may see themselves as one or other of the tiny figures of a bride and groom traditionally placed on a wedding cake. Looking down from the top of the cake may evoke your satisfaction at what you have achieved. A nuptial cake may also represent an important new beginning in your life, and symbolize your excitement at the future. On the other hand, if your dream has you looking up at the towering, multi-tiered wedding cake, this may express the effort that lies ahead in meeting a commitment – marital or otherwise.

369 SALT

Salt, which preserves against decay and corruption, is a symbol of purification and protection. Salt may therefore have a Jungian meaning of taking the individual to a higher plane of perception. When it is shared like bread with visitors, salt is also a symbol of togetherness, evoking perhaps your desire to

SEE ALSO
368:
Wedding
p.157

reconnect with family and friends, or to reach out to people who have been strangers in your life. Spilling salt is popularly said to bring bad luck and, in dreams, may represent some social embarrassment you fear you may have committed.

370 SOCIAL MEALS

A cheerful and convivial meal shared around a table with family, friends or colleagues may reflect feelings of harmony and understanding among whichever of these groups is represented. If it is your family, perhaps some longstanding source of disunity and resentment has finally been dealt with, permitting sought-after closeness and inti-

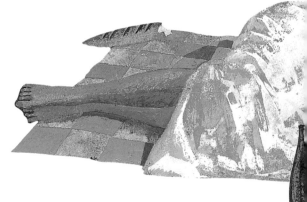

macy. However, meals that are silent and cold may suggest that you feel unable to communicate with or cut off from the people around you.

371 PICNIC
A picnic in the country may express your wish for a life characterized by greater simplicity. You may feel frustrated with conventional formality.

372 CONDIMENTS SET OR SPICE RACK
Bottles standing upright in a condiments set or spice rack may evoke sexual symbolism. Perhaps the dream is expressing a latent need to inject some excitement into your sexual relationship.

VACATIONS AND RELAXATION

373 VACATION TRAVEL

Travelling toward a vacation destination may suggest discontent with the pattern of your current life. Making a hectic dash for the airport or casually sipping champagne in an executive-class lounge can point to whether you are feeling anxious or calm about important professional or personal changes you may be planning.

374 PACKING

Dreamers often find themselves packing for a vacation with many more bags than they would ever use in their waking life. Over-packing may suggest a perverse insistence on clinging to the problems that burden our inner lives.

375 BAGGAGE

Baggage may symbolize our material and psychological preoccupations. Deciding to set upon a journey with no baggage at all expresses a life-enhancing realization that it could be time to leave your "emotional baggage" behind and move on.

SEE ALSO
376: Swimming
p.135

376 BATHING

Bathing, especially when it is done in the soothing atmosphere of a vacation, lends itself naturally to a

Freudian interpretation as a dream-symbol of birth – a desire to float again in the mother's womb.

377 BEACH
Far from being a place of relaxation, the beach may present a disturbing arena for our many anxieties. Freudians might view the dream-game of burying Daddy in the sand as an Oedipal murder, while castration-anxiety may find expression in a sandcastle's tall phallic towers – washed away by the incoming tide of the female or maternal sea.

378 ARBOUR
Vacation-dreams often picture erotic encounters in the romantic setting of an arbour or other sheltered place (such as a wind-break, or cave set into the rocks). In this vision of idyllic sexuality, we may be expressing frustration with aspects of our current relationship, or perhaps seeking thrills akin to those of the holiday romance, with its sense of adventure and freedom from everyday responsibilities.

379 TROUBLES ON VACATION
A dream of a vacation as one disaster after another – troubles with the hotel reservation, poor food, bad weather – can signal a fundamental pessimism that may explain your inability to break out of the habitual

stresses of daily life. But this may alternatively be a lesson warning against over-idealizing how your life might be if you were to make abrupt and radical changes.

380 DESERT ISLAND

A dream of apparently blissful tranquillity on an isolated and uninhabited island may express an urge to run away from the problems of your waking life. Standing on an island set in a vast ocean may symbolize the fact that you prefer to remain on the firmness of the shore (in your conscious mind) rather than to venture into the perilous sea (your unconscious mind) – although, being on an island, you are unable to ignore the presence of the deep and turbulent waters.

A desert island may also represent a sense of isolation or abandonment that may be connected to bereavement, the end of a relationship

SEE ALSO
380: **LOSS AND BEREAVEMENT**
pp.55–57,
The sea p.284

or to a general sense of emotional insecurity. On the other hand, the desert island may express our yearning for solitude, a desire to work out problems without the help of others. Such islands also present a stripped-down innocence, simplicity, and a clarity of thought made possible by the absence of social or technological distractions.

FESTIVALS AND RITUALS

381 CORONATION

Dreams in which we are present at a royal coronation may evoke the exaltation of artistic or intellectual creativity or our striving for a higher spiritual endeavour. If you yourself are the monarch being crowned, this may be a sign of excessive vanity or egotism – especially if, like Napoleon, you place the glittering crown on your own head.

382 RECEIVING AN AWARD

Jungians might interpret dreams of being awarded for achievement or bravery by the president or a monarch, or of receiving a medal in an international sports event, as expressing a desire to identify with an archetypal hero figure (see p.16). On the other hand, such self-aggrandisement might point to an underlying insecurity and low self-esteem – in reality you are unsure of your self-image and feel unable to cope with anything less than universal, uncritical acclaim.

383 FERTILITY RITES

Jungians say that images from fertility rites turn up in modern dreams as part of a "collective unconscious". Dream images such as harvested corn or sacrificial offerings to fertility gods or goddesses may, in such cases, represent a desire to bring about a spiritual rebirth from the symbolic death of the past. For Freudians, individuals who often dream of symbols associated with fertility are probably preoccupied with pregnancy, either their own or their partner's.

384 WEDDING

As a Jungian archetypal image, a wedding may symbolize the union of the male and female aspects of the personality or a union of life's creative forces – reason and fantasy, matter and spirit. Modern interpreters are perhaps more likely to see in wedding-dreams a positive affirmation of enduring family ties.

However, dreaming of no guests at a wedding could express your anxieties about a forthcoming union and, in particular, its social acceptablity to one or other of the two families. The absence of the bride or bridegroom can express lingering doubts and insecurities about your partner's commitment; if someone loses the **wedding ring (385)** this could indicate similar anxieties. As a Freudian female-genital symbol, the ring may also express worries about marital sex.

386 SACRIFICE

Dreams featuring the sacrifice of a human victim may evoke the death of a loved one. A ritual sacrifice may enable mourners to see in the death an opportunity for a new, freer life for themselves.

SEE ALSO
384: **Wedding cake** p.149;
385: **Ring** p.84

387 HALLOWEEN

Halloween derives from an ancient festival of transformation when the boundaries between matter and spirit, life and death became blurred. As such, when it occurs in our dreams, it may represent some profound shift in our emotions or psychology. The licensed childish mischief of modern Halloween celebrations may indicate a desire to rebel against authority-figures, perhaps revealing unsuspected hostility toward them. From the panoply of ghosts, witches, hobgoblins, black cats, sprites and demons, Jungians offer a wide range of archetypal mythical images through which dreamers can explore the darker sides of their unconscious. Freudians need no more than witches riding broomsticks through the night sky to point out Halloween's sexual symbolism.

SEE ALSO
387: **Wearing a mask** p.23, **Cat** p.322, **Symbols of death** p.108; 388: **Social meals** p.150

388 YULE LOG

The old tradition of the Yule log is a relic of a Norse pagan midwinter festival to welcome back the light of the sun after the shortest day. Amid great joy and revelry, the log was placed on the hearth on Christmas Eve and lit with a brand from the previous year's log. As a symbol of warmth in the middle of our darkest, coldest days, the dream-image expresses the need for family solidarity.

389 AND 390 HOLY COMMUNION AND BAPTISM

The Christian sacrament of **eucharist or holy communion (389)** may symbolize union between matter and spirit in the unconscious, or simply a desire to move closer to God.

Baptism (390), a sacrament and rite of passage signifying our acceptance into the wider spiritual community beyond our own close family, may reveal ambivalent attitudes to our parents. On the other hand, it may express a desire for new beginnings and new obligations.

391 BAR MITZVAH OR BAT MITZVAH

For Freud, the bar mitzvah, the Jewish rite of passage for 13-year-old boys, contained strong Oedipal symbolism: with the traditional speech beginning, "Today, I am a man," the boy declares his rivalry toward his father. He then opens the dancing at the party by dancing with his mother. The symbolism is reversed for the bat mitzvah, the girls' ceremony. In dreams, such episodes will be mostly concerned with ambivalent family relationships.

392 CIRCUMCISION

Freud saw the circumcision of young Jews and Muslims as a "ritual substitute" for castration. In his terms, the image may symbolize the father's "pre-emptive strike" against his son's rivalry for the mother's affections.

ART, MUSIC AND DANCE

393 ARTIST

The unfathomable nature of artistic achievement – declared by Freud to be "psychoanalytically inaccessible" – has made the artist the dreamer's symbol of universal mysteries. As writer, painter, composer or sculptor, the artist reaches insights into the human condition by intuition rather than scientifically measurable analysis. Thus, he or she provides a role model for individual initiative in the dreamer's own personal creativity, artistic or otherwise.

394 AND 395 WORKS OF ART

The quality attributed to a **painting (394)** can indicate the progress the dreamer is making with their artistic or other creative ambitions. A picture defaced before completion may evoke feelings of creative and even sexual impotence. The pigments used, whether bright and vibrant or dull and gloomy, may provide clues to your emotional state. In dreams of portrait-paintings, a smile or frown, for example, can indicate what we think the subject feels about us – or it may reflect our own current mood, if it is a self-portrait.

A **drawing (395)** might be sketchier or more provisional than a painting and perhaps its message should be viewed more tentatively. In portrait-drawings, if the (phallic) pen or pencil is prominent or especially vivid, Freudians would say that the dreamer desires intercourse with the subject of the portrait.

396 SCULPTURE

Its three-dimensional, tactile qualities make sculpture the most physically sensual of the visual arts. Dreams can heighten the pleasure of touching a sculpture, which may even come to life and reach out to touch the dreamer. Such dreams recall the Greek myth of Pygmalion, who sculpts a statue named Galatea that embodies his ideal of womanhood. The goddess of love, Aphrodite, brings Galatea to life and Pygmalion marries her. However, the dream may be a reminder that in reality if we over-idealize the opposite sex in general, or one person in particular, the ideal will remain beyond our grasp where we have chosen to place it – on a pedestal.

397 EXHIBITION

An art exhibition is an act of exposing yourself to the public gaze. Dreams may convey this act of exposure by showing the artist walking naked through a gallery, suggesting feelings of vulnerability in connection with some cherished project.

SEE ALSO
394: **Bright colours** p.33, **Talking paintings** p.351; 396: **One object into another** p.352

398 MUSEUM

The museum often appears as a venerable guardian of humankind's creative past. It is also a symbol of stasis and stagnation. A hubbub disrupting the museum's hallowed silence may express a desire to desanctify artistic conventions and, perhaps, make creativity accessible to all – or, more particularly, to oneself.

399 AUCTION

Bidders taking part in an art auction may be those whom you feel place a value on your creativity. Do you feel judged by someone in your life? The successful bidder may be your judge, or someone else from whom you are seeking approval, such as a parent, colleague or loved one.

400 MUSIC

Music can be the most immediately emotionally evocative of all the arts. Sublime and ethereal church music may symbolize our striving for creativity, and our spiritual progress. Earthy folk music or raucous rock and roll, on the other hand, suggest the more rawly passionate and down-to-earth sides of your nature. A cacophony may reflect current disharmony in a personal or professional relationship.

SEE ALSO
400: **Churches** p.49, **Melody** p.345, **Mozart** p.366, **Beethoven** p.366, **Singing** p.168

art, music and dance 163

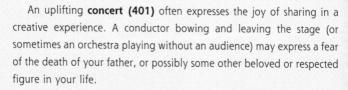

An uplifting **concert (401)** often expresses the joy of sharing in a creative experience. A conductor bowing and leaving the stage (or sometimes an orchestra playing without an audience) may express a fear of the death of your father, or possibly some other beloved or respected figure in your life.

402 WIND INSTRUMENTS

However pure and unearthly music itself may be, instruments by their shape and the manner in which they are played may possess a distinct physical symbolism. For Freud, for example, wind instruments played vertically (oboes, clarinets and so on) are associated with oral sex. Jungians relate pipes and reed instruments to Pan, Greek god of fertility and the wild outdoors – the sounds they make embody primal energies.

SEE ALSO
402: **Flute**
p.166, **Fife**
p.166; 405: **Fife**
p.166; 408:
Churches p.49,
Wedding p.157

403 AND 404 STRING INSTRUMENTS

The shape of the **violin (403)** and other orchestral string instruments evokes the female body and playing them – especially the **cello (404)** – may therefore represent a symbolic act of sex. The violin that popular legend attributes to Emperor Nero (he is said to have been fiddling while Rome burned), has a dream-association of heartless irresponsibility.

405 DRUM

Drums beating may represent the primordial rhythms of life, such as the heartbeat and the motions of sex. As an instrument accompanying men going to war, drums may also express our more aggressive instincts.

406 HARP

One of music's most ancient instruments (known in Egypt at least 5,000 years ago), the harp is traditionally the instrument of gods and angels. In dreams, it is likely to be playing celestial music evocative of the sleeper's desire for peace and harmony. The music is also sometimes plaintive, symbolizing, it is said, a happiness not to be found on this earth – and therefore perhaps suggesting a death-wish.

407 PIANO

The piano frequently appears in dreams playing on its own. The black piano with its black-and-white keys may symbolize the death of the person that the dreamer will identify as the absent pianist.

408 ORGAN

Organs are associated with sacred rituals, especially weddings and funerals. Dreams of organ music, therefore, can express a desire for commitment, or alternatively fear of death.

409 FLUTE

The flute is the instrument of goatherds and their lusty goat-horned god Pan, which gives it strongly sexual connotations. Whether to charm snakes out of their baskets or children from their homes to follow the Pied Piper of Hamelin, the flute is often linked with seductiveness in dream-symbolism. The **fife (410)** is a little flute for playing cheerful and jaunty tunes, yet traditionally it has been used to call men to war. The instrument may disguise a feeling of hostility toward someone or represent the courage necessary to face great difficulties in life.

411 TRUMPETS

A trumpet may be fanfaring a great success or a momentous event in the dreamer's life. Or they may be a warning of impending disaster. Trumpets brought down the walls of Jericho and are supposed to herald the Day of Judgment. The dream-trumpet could be a wake-up call to embark on a major project too long delayed.

412 DANCE

SEE ALSO
409: **Drum**
p.165

For Jungians and Freudians alike, most dancing dreams represent in symbolic form sexual courtship or intercourse itself. Dancing in an uncontrolled frenzy may evoke an explosive desire to achieve unity between body and spirit, an artistic or spiritual bond with the infinite. On the other hand, the uninhibited enjoyment of **disco dancing (413)** is less likely to express a lofty spiritual aspiration than your desire to satisfy a perhaps over-heated sexual appetite.

A dream of **ballet (414)** may sublimate in elegant stylized form some disturbing, perhaps even brutal emotions. The dreamer may discover a need to confront rage or hatred felt toward someone.

415 FANCY DRESS BALL

A social event at which those present are in disguise, including yourself, may reveal your perceptiveness about the roles people choose to adopt in public, reflected in the costumes they are wearing. Or perhaps the costumes are an indication of their true nature? Don't forget to take note of your own costume, too.

416 PROCESSION

A procession may appear either as a grand and grave occasion, a splendid state pageant, or as a flamboyant Mardi Gras parade. Dreamers seeing themselves among dignitaries in a solemn procession may discover unsuspected pretensions. A joyous parade presents a more reassuring self-image of being at ease and feeling thoroughly at home in your skin.

417 SINGING

Singing may represent a gesture of praise to a higher being (mortal or otherwise), a celebratory hymn or an act of mourning. A dream-song may also be a profession of love.

A **choir (418)**, naturally, may be a symbol of uplifting or heavenly song, and dreamers may express in the image of a choir the need to share with others strong feelings of sorrow or joy. ★

SEE ALSO
415: **Wearing a mask** p.23; 417: **Churches** p.49

PLAY

419 TOYS

Toys – trains, planes, cars and animals – may represent a wish to return to a child's perspective and a world over which you can assert control. This may occur at a time when you are having difficulties coping with problems in the adult world. Breaking toys may express your frustration with problems that resist an easy solution.

420 DOLLS

The way a child plays with a male or female doll can offer an intriguing insight into how they perceive their relationship with their parents. Similarly, adult doll-dreams may reflect our deep-seated beliefs about or feelings toward our parents. If you are a new parent who dreams of dolls, the dream may be expressing your anxiety about repeating unhappy patterns of parental behaviour with your own child.

421 PUPPETS

If toy-dreams focus on asserting control over problems, puppet-dreams are about asserting control over people. You may be the puppet that is being manipulated – by a person close to you or a work colleague – or a puppeteer who does the manipulating, but of whom?

422 BOARD GAMES

Games in which pieces move around a playing-board at the throw of the dice are often designed to mirror life's progress and pitfalls, and this is often what they symbolize in dreams, reflecting our anxieties about the chances of personal failure, as well as a fear of factors beyond our control. Specific games may have their own symbolism – for example, sin and sexuality in Snakes and Ladders.

423 CHESS

The ancient game of chess is rich with the symbolism of sexual rivalry and fundamental dualities, such as male and female, life and death. Chess is won by killing the father–king (the word "checkmate" comes from the Persian for "the king is dead"). The piece most capable of killing him is the mother–queen. Humble pawns find strength only by acting together. The game is a battle between light and dark, possibly representing a dilemma in which our higher moral integrity contends with baser motives – very commonly where money is involved: the person buying your house hasn't spotted the damp patch, do you mention it?

In Jungian terms, the game of chess can stand for the dreamer's conscious (white pieces) and unconscious (black pieces) minds contending for supremacy.

424 BACKGAMMON

The backgammon board is divided into two halves known as the "inner" and "outer tables" which may symbolize the unconscious and conscious mind. The game's object, to be the first player to remove all your pieces from the outer table to the inner table and then off the board altogether, may point to your desire to discover or resolve the secrets of your unconscious before the other player – death? – stops you.

425 DICE

Supreme symbol of chance, dice suggest that a dreamer may feel that random factors rather than their own abilities could determine an important event in their personal or professional life. For those unconvinced by Einstein's belief that "God does not play dice," the dream may also reflect doubts that the universe itself is subject to anything but the forces of chance.

SEE ALSO
422: **Snake** p.328, **Ladder** p.116; 423: **Pair of masks** p.80; 426: **Prizes** p.25, **Hoarding money** p.199

426 LOTTERY

Winning a lottery is a common wish-fulfilment dream in the modern world. A prize of money may symbolize an important life-goal, but if you hope to attain this goal without effort your expectations may be unrealistic. Freudians relate money-dreams to anal preoccupations, and the lottery could suggest the dreamer's desire to break with "anally retentive" stinginess.

427 WAGER OR BET

Making any kind of wager or bet, perhaps at a bookmaker's or casino, most obviously may stand for some gamble or risky venture we are considering, whether in business or in our private life. Are we risking too much? Have we weighed up all the odds?

428 FORTUNE-TELLING

To dream of a fortune-telling could reveal concerns about your individual identity and future prospects. Your response to any "prophecy" given in the dream would depend on your personal attitude to fortune-telling itself. If you are a natural skeptic, such a dream might suggest an imminent crisis of faith in the rule of reason.

429 SPORTS ARENA

Sports can symbolize personal achievement in any sphere. The formal context of an arena might signify rivalry with colleagues or a need for social approval.

430 BOXING

The violence of boxing can reveal considerable hostility toward an opponent, expressing an enduring sibling rivalry with a brother, with the referee as father-figure. A knock-out inflicted on the dreamer may denote a guilt-laden wish to inflict self-punishment.

431 BASEBALL

This all-American game offers a wealth of phallic and other sexual symbols – the dreams may be littered with symbols such as the bat, the ball, the gloves or the long-peaked cap. The traditional Freudian view of dream-baseball as an Oedipal activity is demonstrated by the players' fierce challenges to the father-umpire.

432 CRICKET

The friendly competition and summery associations of the quintessential English game – at least in its traditional, amateur form – can reveal a desire to withdraw from a more fiercely competitive environment, such as work, or family in-fighting. The white outfits may express a yearning for innocence.

SEE ALSO
428: **Gipsies** p.89; 430: **Brother or sister** p.93

433 FOOTBALL

The high passions of football – whether in the form of the American game, soccer or rugby – may express considerable sexual excitement for the dreamer. A goal may symbolize orgasm, just as a near miss may represent fears of impotence. Jungians may prefer to see the dreamer's success or failure in terms of spiritual aspirations.

434 FENCING

Dreamers can scarcely ignore the sexual symbolism of the thrusting and parrying of fencing. The dream's most significant moment might well be when the duelers take off their fencing-masks to reveal just whom the dreamer is "fighting" – a lover or perhaps a parent – or your own unconscious urges. Does the stylized fight to the death disguise a genuine hostility?

SEE ALSO

434: **Pair of masks** p.80; 435: **Whips** p.46, **Horse** p.327, **Toys** p.169; 439: **The sea** p.284, **Water** p.284

435 HORSE RACE

The rhythmic gallop of a horse race may symbolize sexual intercourse, but with the added emotional weight of triumph or failure at the "winning post". Whipping the horse may reveal unsuspected sadomasochistic feelings. A race watched through binoculars may indicate a tendency to voyeurism.

A **rocking horse (436)** may bear the same sexual connotations as a real horse, but of course it can also express our yearning for childhood pleasures and securities, embodied in the comforting rocking motion.

437 SKATING

Skating-dreams may present a desire to embark on some daring venture. Dreamers may imagine themselves performing with grace and an unfamiliar new feeling of freedom, although they should be aware of the metaphorical sense of the phrase, "skating on thin ice".

438 SKIING

Going down a mountain is a classic Freudian symbol of sexual intercourse to which the elated sensations of skiing add a thrilling dimension. Skiing dreams are often coupled with a sense of falling that may complicate the sexual thrill with overlay of anxiety, perhaps suggesting guilt at illicit sexual feelings.

439 REGATTA OR YACHTING

Dreams of a sailing or boating regatta may, in the Jungian view, suggest exploration of the collective unconscious. For Freudians, the yachts may be the dreamer harking back to the time when he made his or her way through the mother's womb.

440 AND 441 PLAYGROUND

Swings (440) are an image of childhood freedom and excitement expressing a feeling akin to that of flying. If, as Freudians claim, the rhythmical motion of swinging connotes sexual intercourse, the presence of someone we know to give the swing a push may indicate the object of our desire. Dreams of straddling a **seesaw (441)** may also have sexual connotations.

442 CAROUSEL

The merry-go-round began as a mechanical model of grand royal caval-cades. In dreams, it reproduces the sexual symbolism associated both with horses and with flying. The carousel dream may express a desire to return to the sexual innocence of childhood.

443 SPINNING TOP

The spinning top is one of the most ancient and universal of toys. The wailing sound it produces may be associated with bereavement. The hypnotic nature of the top's spinning motion may also suggest the trance-like or meditative state in which we look into the depths of the unconscious.

SEE ALSO
440: **Riding** p.134, **Flying unaided** p.119;
442: **Rocking horse** p.175, **Horse race** p.174, **Horse** p.327, **Toys** p.169

TRANSACTIONS

FIGHTING AND VIOLENCE

444 VIOLENCE TO THE SELF

Seeing yourself as a victim of self-inflicted violence suggests guilt and self-blame, perhaps related to the death of a loved one or the break-up of a relationship, which we feel – probably wrongly – may have been avoidable if only we had acted sooner. Such dream-violence may also express low self-esteem, even self-loathing, manifested in unconscious destructive urges that we should deal with before they erupt into our waking lives.

445 VIOLENCE TOWARD OTHERS

A dreamer lashing out indiscriminately at others around them may be struggling to fight undesirable impulses in their conscious or unconscious minds. Violence against an older person can suggest resistance to a figure of authority. Violence toward one or more children may express the dreamer's inability to accept the child in themselves.

> **SEE ALSO**
> 444: **Enemy** p.183; 445: **Fist fight, Struggle** p.185; 446: **Guns** p.47, **Artillery** p.183

446 MALFUNCTIONING WEAPON

Firearms or other weapons that fail to work may indicate anxiety about sexual performance, or, more broadly, the malfunction may evoke the dreamer's sense of powerlessness to handle challenges.

Weapons that do function properly may express the aggressive side of male sexuality, or else may suggest an inability to deal with people or express ideas other than in an authoritarian manner.

447 KILLING

A dream of people or animals being killed need not be prompted by latent violent tendencies. For dreamers undergoing analysis or otherwise seeking to take more control over their lives, it may express

the weakening of ingrained modes of thought and action that have been restricting your personal growth. A deliberate act of **murder (448)** more probably suggests hostility, the precise significance depending on the identity of both assailant and victim. Assuming no genuine homicidal wish-fulfilment is present, killing a figure of authority suggests a desire to escape social or personal constraints. Slaying a parent points to some unresolved issue from childhood, perhaps even a still-resented act of parental discipline. If the parent is of the opposite sex, Freud might view the dream as evidence of an Oedipus or Electra complex.

449 WARS AND BATTLES

Warfare may symbolize a dramatic conflict between elements in the conscious and unconscious areas of the dreamer's mind. The battle classically pitches a conscious demand for order against the instinctive urge of the unconscious to rebel. The dream may signal a need for a conciliatory peace settlement – an acknowledgment and acceptance of our darker side rather than a futile attempt to drive it out.

450 TANK

With its turret and cannon, the tank is among the most aggressive of phallic symbols. The dream image projects our fears of (or perhaps even our subliminal desire for) violent sexuality. Extended to the realm of ideas, the tank could symbolize an attack on convention, indiscriminately flattening accepted principles and all those who defend them.

451 TORPEDO

By its shape a torpedo symbolizes male sexuality. Its function is to deliver an explosion by stealth, so the dream may express a wish for clandestine, illicit sex. The torpedo's passage through water, a symbol of the mother, may suggest incestuous desire.

452 AND 453 ARTILLERY

The huge firepower of a modern high-tech **missile (452)** presents a variation of the phallic symbol, as does a traditional **cannon or field gun (453)**. Outside the sexual sphere, such weaponry may symbolize the obstacles you feel ranged against you as you pursue your aspirations – especially, perhaps, if you are a woman in a traditionally male profession. Who are the "big shots" barring your progress?

454 ENEMY

A figure who appears as your bitter foe may be none other than the Shadow side of your own

SEE ALSO
451: **Water, The sea** p.284;
453: **Guns** p.47;
454: **Being chased** p.29,
Intimate strangers p.30,
Violence to the self p.180

personality, confronting you with your prejudices and other unwelcome sides of your nature. If the enemy is clearly identifiable as someone you know, the dream may reveal your hitherto unsuspected feelings of animosity or distrust toward that person.

455 FIST FIGHT

A bareknuckle fight between a younger and older person may derive from rivalry between the dreamer and a parent, or a more general resentment of authority. A fight between individuals of the same generation may point to sibling rivalry.

Similar interpretations may apply to any other sort of **struggle (456)** between two individuals. Such a struggle is often a fight for freedom. You may be resisting the difficult path of truth or spiritual striving, as Jacob wrestled with the angel of God in the Bible. Like a fist fight, the struggle may be viewed by Freudians as a contest with your father or mother for the affections of the other parent.

457 AXE

An axe or hatchet may be creative rather than destructive, its cleaving action symbolically signalling a readiness to separate the valuable from the worthless, or to find a way through an emotional

SEE ALSO
455: **Boxing**
p.173; 456:
Cripple p.99

impasse. Wielding a hatchet may point to your determination to "cut out the dead wood" and free yourself from some person or thing that is holding you back. An executioner's axe may symbolize your tendency for excessive self-criticism and self-condemnation.

458 AND 459 BLADED WEAPONS

The **Dagger (458)** is the classic instrument of furtive assassinations and may indicate a passionate but concealed hostility toward another. Often worn as a mainly ceremonial or decorative item of male regalia (for example, in traditional Scottish dress), a dagger symbolizes masculine self-esteem but not necessarily violence, and may stand for the secure, protective presence of the dreamer's father.

The emblematic weapon of chivalry, the **sword (459)** is the instrument of the archetypal Hero (see p.16). Wielded by the angel that barred Adam and Eve's return to Eden, a flaming sword is an ancient symbol of tribulation, perhaps evoking feelings of remorse.

SEE ALSO
458, 459:
Knife p.47,
Sacrifice
p.157;
459: **Knight**
p.85

460 BOW AND ARROW

The bow can symbolize the tension with which we hold in check the arrow of our unconscious desires. Most often, in keeping with the traditional weapon of Cupid, god of love, such desires are erotic. However, firing the arrow into the skies rather than at an earthly target can express our wish to dedicate our energies to some higher purpose.

461 MUSHROOM CLOUD

The baleful, doom-laden nuclear bomb cloud is a terrifying image of utter destruction. However, its mushroom form may also represent regeneration: mushrooms thrive in an environment of decomposed matter, life growing from death.

TESTS AND EXAMINATIONS

462 EXAMINATIONS

Anxiety-filled exam dreams continue to crop up long after our school and college years have become a distant memory. A feeling of powerlessness to shape our own destiny may be behind a dream in which we hurry – often late – down endless corridors to find the examination room, or in which we hand in a blank paper at the end of the exam. Another common dream involves turning up naked to an exam, which may point to our fear of social humiliation.

463 FACING AN INTERVIEW PANEL

Facing an oral examination can be the most fretful of all anxiety-dreams. A stern panel may seem to probe your innermost feelings with relentless

questions. Your hesitation or tongue-tied silence before the panel may reflect a refusal to confront feelings that demand to be expressed. Such dreams may point to a difficult relationship with, for example, a parent who is what psychologists call an "interrogator", always probing and asking questions, denying you privacy and in doing so often undermining your self-esteem by leading you to feel that they do not trust you.

Conducting an interview (464) might enable you to turn the tables on an authority figure who has usually played the inquisitorial role in your life. While expressing a need for revenge, the dream could also reveal, by implication, your shaky self-esteem.

465 FILLING OUT FORMS

A dream of filling out forms may present a list of unintelligible questions. We may feel helpless in the face of current anxieties, perhaps about money. The dream could also express our instinct that some current enterprise in our life is not the right direction for us to be taking.

466 RESULTS POSTED

Perceived failure may be reflected in a dream of not finding our name on a list of those who have passed a school exam. Or perhaps we feel that someone is deliberately marking us down?

SEE ALSO
465: **Bureau-cracy** p.35

GIVING AND RECEIVING

467 GIFTS

Giving a present usually symbolizes a need to express love or consideration for another person, whereas receiving a gift is an indication of an individual's perceived standing in society. Receiving a shower of gifts suggests that we feel we are held in esteem.

A dream of **unexpected gifts (468)** can have several meanings. If you have been feeling unloved or perhaps emotionally bruised after a relationship break-up, the gift can point to a recognition of your own worth. If you are the giver, the dream may be a warning to present personal qualities in a more honest or straightforward way, so that you do not catch others off their guard.

An inappropriate gift of something that you actively dislike or otherwise have no use for may express your feeling that somebody's attentions are not entirely welcome.

SEE ALSO
470: **Red rose** p.46,
COLOURS pp.341–343;
471: **Hoarding money** p.199

469 UNPLEASANT GIFTS

A dream in which you open a beautiful gift box to find rotten, foul-smelling food or some other disgusting contents indicates disappointed expectations. The image may reveal your intuition that someone's apparently good intentions may disguise a selfish ulterior motive.

470 BOUQUET OF FLOWERS

In dreams as in waking life, the gift of a bouquet of flowers is one of the commonest symbols of love or affection. The shade of the flowers may be significant: for example, red flowers may symbolize the female sexual organs, but white blooms evoke an image of innocence or virginity. Like the dream-gift which, on being opened, turns out to be something unpleasant, a decaying bouquet suggests the recipient's disappointed expectations.

471 BOX OF CHOCOLATES

A gift of chocolate may hark back to the dreamer's childhood and infantile oral pleasures. In Freudian terms chocolate may be a dream-image of excrement, representing an anal fixation that may indicate a tendency to be overly formal or uptight, or mean about money. However, beware of over-analyzing such a dream: as Freud might have said, sometimes chocolates are just chocolates.

472 EMPTY GIFT BOX

The image of a gift box with nothing inside may signify the hollowness of what appear at first sight to be attractive promises. Perhaps you have to face the reality of an unrequited love, or to lower your expectations of what might come out of some current venture.

LETTERS AND PACKAGES

473 MAILMAN/POSTMAN

As the carrier of messages symbolizing new opportunities, a mail delivery man who passes by without a letter may indicate a general or particular disappointment. Dreamers running after the mailman are perhaps expressing a resolution to take decisive action and create their own openings. Dreamers seeing themselves in this role may feel they deserve a position of responsibility and trust.

474 LETTERS

Messages received by mail are often positive symbols at times of new opportunities or unexpected challenges in the dreamer's life. Such dreams may also occur at moments of stagnation in your personal or professional life and may serve as a stimulus.

475 ENVELOPE

For Freud, an envelope is a symbol of female sexuality, and inserting a letter into the envelope represents sexual intercourse. Left unopened, the dream envelope may represent virginity or a woman's denial of her affections to someone.

Leaving a letter in its envelope unread can also suggest the dreamer is unable either to acknowledge a perhaps unpalatable truth or to take advantage of an opportunity offered.

476 UNINTELLIGIBLE LETTER

A letter that is illegible or written in an incomprehensible foreign language may suggest our frustration at not being able to solve some difficult issue. A letter that turns out to be nothing but a blank page can indicate that, rather than waiting in vain for others to offer an opportunity, you should consider taking the initiative yourself.

477 ANONYMOUS LETTER

An anonymous letter can be an alert from the unconscious. Emotions may be in turmoil and the unconscious may be telling you to slow down, take stock and reflect on where you are heading.

SEE ALSO
476: **Inability to understand** p.51;
479: **E-mail error message** p.38

478 POSTCARDS

Postcards are often frivolous and indiscreet, open for anyone to read. Finding someone else reading your postcard may suggest an unconscious desire to be more open with those who mean most to you.

479 E-MAIL

The appearance of e-mail is for many dreamers fraught with new symbolic dangers. Clicking on the "Send" button may suggest having control over your power to make decisions, but clicking too hastily may mean you are communicating, irrevocably, an idea that has not been thought through. Clicking on the "Delete" button may symbolize your desire to remove an uncomfortable idea or person from your conscious mind.

480 PARCELS

In the Freudian view, parcels, like envelopes (and most other containers), may symbolize the female genitalia. The parcel and your feelings about its contents may express your attitude to female sexuality in general, especially if you are a man. The joy of new love may explain why you are excited and cannot wait to open your parcel. However, if you do not want to open it – perhaps afraid that it contains a bomb – this may express a fear of deeply committed relationships with women.

481 DEEDS OR DOCUMENTS

The appearance in dreams of deeds or formal documents – such as birth, marriage and death certificates, wills, and real-estate deeds – may express a preoccupation with a key rite of passage. Burning or otherwise destroying such documents may signal a point of closure.

482 CONTRACT

A contract may symbolize a personal or professional commitment in your waking life about which you may be ambivalent. Tearing up the dream-contract may evoke your strong misgivings about the commitment, but the image may also convey your relief or even exhilaration at being freed from an obligation.

483 BLOT

An ink-blot may suggest that the dreamer has doubts about the validity of opportunities represented by a written communication. As in a psychological Rohrschach test, the shape of the blot may be suggestive. A tear-smudge on the letter may suggest feelings of guilt at causing sadness to the person who has written to us. Or if the tear stain is your own, this may perhaps indicate the emotional difficulty of bringing an end to a relationship.

484 TELEGRAM

The telegram has become a rather old-fashioned medium and its appearance in a dream may be related to a memory from the distant past linked to an important event such as the birth of a baby or a death in the family. A telegram may express an urgent yearning for contact with a long-dead friend or loved one.

SHOPPING AND MONEY

485 STORE/SHOP

The image of a store may be viewed as presenting the range of life's prospects and rewards. How much we are buying in the dream may indicate our ability to take advantage of these prospects. Discovering that the store has sold out of the items we were looking for may express our frustration at not getting what we want out of life. A frequent shopping dream involves the panic of **closing time (486)**. Not being able to buy all we want before we have to leave the store can evoke the anxiety of life being too short for us to fulfil all our ambitions.

487 STORE/SHOP WINDOWS

Window shopping presents enticing opportunities that may be out of reach. The image may evoke frustration or envy that we are missing out on the good things of life, but it may also remind us that we have choices: we can go elsewhere for rewards that are truly accessible and perhaps of greater value.

488 STORE/SHOP COUNTER

A store counter is a place where we make our selections, and as such may feature in the dreams of those who are contemplating a major change in their life. We may be confused by the huge array of

SEE ALSO
485:
BUILDINGS
pp.232–248

possibilities set before us. If the items we covet are too expensive, our subconscious may be warning us against over-ambition.

489 SELLING

Selling is the art of persuasion. We may be trying to "sell" an important project to our colleagues, or conversely deciding whether to "buy" a proposal or an idea. Selling is also about persuading people to buy something that they did not know they wanted, which may suggest we should assess the value of any offer with great care. The ultimate dream-sale may be getting a loved one to accept a proposal of marriage.

490 ODDS AND ENDS

A store selling a wide range of miscellaneous goods – such as buttons, zippers, ribbons, beads, pins and needles – may conjure up all the tiresome little details of everyday life. They are easily overlooked when we are intent on the big picture of our life's ambitions. The dream may be reminding us to pay attention to these small items, without which everything else may come unstitched.

491 PEDLAR OR HAWKER

A street-pedlar is a dream-figure evoking not only freedom as someone working at the outer margins of society, but also dishonesty as a vendor of possibly dubious goods. Dreamers may be weighing the attractions and risks of some new undertaking, or the possible motives of a recent acquaintance.

492 TRADE

Trade symbolizes interaction in a professional, intellectual or sexual relationship. You may be considering what personal qualities you and a prospective partner, colleague or friend have to offer each other.

493 MONEY

For Jung, money appears as a symbol of power, and represents an ability to achieve an objective. For Freud, money is a symbol of excrement and a dream of **hoarding money (494)** expresses an anal fixation perhaps caused by the parents' mishandling of the dreamer's childhood toilet training – and thus may reflect an obsessively orderly and obstinate personality. Dreams of a pile of **coins (495)** present for Freud the most graphic example of money as an expression of anal preoccupations.

> **SEE ALSO**
> 494: **Toilet dreams** p.105;
> 495: **Purses** p.49

Also, of course, dreams of money may simply reflect anxieties about our finances.

496 MARKET

The rich and brightly-hued array of an open-air market, offering a greater profusion of goods than one store, reminds us of the wide world of choices beyond the familiar surroundings of your waking life. The dream may occur at a watershed in your life, such as leaving home, embarking on a new relationship (or ending an old one), or changing jobs. The mingled cries of the street vendors and the clogged commotion of the market alleys may express your fears of losing clarity and direction.

497 BAZAAR

The exotic atmosphere and variety of bright and unusual goods on sale make the image of a typical Middle Eastern type of bazaar a heady symbol of our love of travel or our general desire to seek new and exciting experiences. On the other hand, the closed-in, warren-like lanes may evoke feelings of claustrophobia or panic, while the haggling and persistence of importunate merchants may represent people in our lives whom we find either intimidating or excessively demanding.

SEE ALSO
496: **Raft** p.24;
497: **Unfamiliar surroundings** p.21

498 BILL OR CHECK

A demand for payment confronts us with the investment of personal resources we need to make in order to progress. The amount may come as a shock, but the size of the bill may be the measure of what we could get out of life. **Making a payment (499)** is always the hard part and can be even harder in a dream: we may find our pockets empty or our credit cards rejected. Thwarted-payment dreams may highlight feelings of inadequacy and seem to be a form of self-punishment. They also emphasize the effort necessary to achieve personal goals: if you put nothing in, you are unlikely to get anything out. But beware, too, of squandering valuable resources. **Paying with hard cash (500)** rather than by check or credit card may represent your impatience to take advantage of an opportunity with unrealistic haste.

Receiving payment (501) may reflect our sense that we are being rewarded for our efforts in some sphere of endeavour – which may be spiritual or emotional as much as material.

502 SAFE OR STRONGBOX

As a secure container of valuables, a safe may symbolize female sexuality. As a place for hoarding, it may also be an image of avarice, which may indicate an excessively orderly and inflexible approach to life. Given that money is a Jungian symbol of the power to achieve spiritual objectives, the safe can also represent the storehouse of insights we need to accumulate for self-fulfilment.

503 RENT

A house is often said to symbolize the self. To pay the rent is thus to preserve the integrity of the self – against, for example, an overbearing parent, represented by the person to whom the rent is due. On the other hand, if the dream emphasizes the fact that you are merely a tenant and not the house's owner, this may reflect a lack of ease with yourself or your body.

504 PAWNBROKER

Dreamers leaving treasured possessions with a pawnbroker may be sacrificing one set of values of which they are proud in order to attain some uncertain objective. The figure of the pawnbroker represents the undervaluation of our talents, achievements or experience and may also stand for someone whom we perhaps revere but whose advice is questionable.

SEE ALSO

502: **Trunk, chest or box** p.242, **Lock and key** p.114; 503: **Landlord or landlady** p.97, **House** p.237

505 STOCK MARKET CRASH

A dream of a disaster on the financial markets may involve the image of a ruined banker or stockbroker committing suicide by shooting himself or jumping from a high window. The dreamer is perhaps expressing feelings of deep personal disappointment prompted by the failure of a marriage or of some other venture in which they feel they have "invested" too much of their time and energy.

COMMUNICATION

506 DISAGREEMENT

The airing of a disagreement can reveal your doubts about hitherto deeply held convictions: the dialogue that appears in the dream is a dramatization of your own inner conflict. However, this can signal a constructive moment in your personal development, an openness to testing new ideas in the light of experience.

SEE ALSO

507: **Struggle** p.185; 508: **Law court** p.232, **Plaintiff** p.209

507 QUARREL

A full-blown quarrel in a dream can be inspired by strong feelings of frustration in your waking life,

especially if your dream-persona finds him- or herself unable to win over the other participant, despite repeating the same arguments again and again. Such a dream may also suggest a sense of inadequacy in communicating any arguments at all. You may of course be attributing this failing to the other person involved in the quarrel.

508 LAWSUIT

Conducting legal proceedings against a person or group of people may express a need to win their approval. The lawsuit may also suggest the dreamer's secret and perhaps unconscious desire to punish or humiliate people who do not agree with them.

509 MAKING A SPEECH

Standing up and addressing an audience may express a sense that we feel misunderstood by the world or by those around us and want to set the record straight. A rousing round of applause for our speech may be a wish-fulfilment, symbolizing the approval or acceptance that we feel denied in our waking life.

510 UNRULY AUDIENCE

The image of an unruly audience can indicate, in the refusal of others to listen, our resentment that our arguments are not being listened to or taken seriously, or that our valid efforts are not being recognized. The yelling and catcalling mob at our feet may reflect our own true feelings toward other people in general – are we guilty of believing ourselves to be "above the crowd"?

A noisy, restive audience may also appear as a means of disguising one particular troubling person in our lives who might otherwise stand out.

SEE ALSO
510: **Parliaments** p.36;
512: **Train entering tunnel** p.45

LAW AND ORDER

511 THIEF OR ROBBER

The person who steals people's valuables may represent someone whom we distrust without necessarily realizing the fact. If our dream-self is the thief, the object we steal may affect the dream's meaning – symbols of female sexual organs like a purse or handbag, or phallic symbols like a weapon or a car, may suggest a temptation to commit adultery. A **train robbery (512)** includes another common phallic symbol and may indicate, for male dreamers, a fear of impotence. Being robbed at gunpoint or knifepoint expresses our normal fears of violence, and in particular sexual violation. A **highwayman (513)** may reflect the dreamer's illicit

desires and deepest fears, but as an expression of freedom or an impatience with social conventions.

Since a pocket may be a Freudian symbol for female genitalia, a **pickpocket (514)** may stand for an illicit sexual act. Breaking down doors and entering a building, a **burglar (515)** may be acting out our fears of sexual violation, or of letting people in on our private emotions.

516 BAILIFF

Like the summons to appear in court, the arrival at your door of a bailiff who has come to confiscate your property may express a sense that you have not fulfilled your obligations in some sphere of your life – or perhaps you are generally worried about money. On the other hand, the dream may reveal your true feelings toward material success: perhaps you would secretly prefer to avoid the frustrations involved in striving for materialistic goals?

517 TRIAL

A dream of a trial in court may symbolize the dreamer's preoccupations with the oppressive constraints of society, embodied in its bureaucracy and authoritarian institutions. If we know the person on trial, the dream may serve as a reminder to give greater consideration to the problems of people close to us who may be going through a difficult period.

518 SUBPOENA OR SUMMONS

Receiving an order to appear in court can represent your guilt over an area of personal or business affairs that you may have been neglecting recently. However, a dream-summons may be a call for you to act as a witness for the defence – is there a cause or individual in your waking life that you feel may need your support?

519 LAWYER

The person who speaks for us before the court may embody the supportive friend or relative whom we need in a time of stress. Strong counsel, however, may also indicate that we are becoming too dependent and are losing control of our own affairs.

520 PLAINTIFF

A dream in which we act as plaintiff, suing the perpetrator of some perceived injury or injustice, may arise from feelings of paranoia or self-pity. An unsuccessful legal action gives our sense of paranoia even greater opportunity to express itself.

Winning the case and seeing the defendant punished, far from being a positive image, may point to feelings of vindictiveness and self-righteousness.

SEE ALSO
515: **House** p.237; 517, 518, 519, 520: **Defendant in court** p.37, **Law court** p.232, **Lawsuit** p.205

521 JURY

The members of a dream-jury may be those we suspect will decide our future, especially if their faces are familiar – loved ones, colleagues, friends. But the dream may possibly reveal our fear that we are being judged by those close to us. Unknown faces suggest a feeling that our fate is out of our control. If one or even all twelve faces are our own, the dream indicates that we have the power to decide for ourselves.

522 VERDICT

A verdict, whether positive or negative, often represents our own judgment on ourselves. A stern judge delivering the verdict – and, if guilty, the sentence – may represent a judgmental or controlling father.

523 MISBEHAVIOUR

Dreams of misbehaviour as an adult – deliberately breaking something, giggling during a church service or other solemn occasion, or throwing a temper tantrum – are a scarcely disguised throwback to childhood rebellion against parental restrictions. Such dreams of childish naughtiness can express a healthy creative urge to resist being suffocated by convention.

SEE ALSO
521, 522:
Defendant in court p.37,
Law court p.232

524 CRIME

Dreaming of yourself as a criminal may not indicate any malicious intent but may simply reflect feelings of guilt or a general desire to rebel against social or peer-group conventions. In Freudian terms, a one-on-one attack may reflect sibling rivalry or the Oedipal crime of patricide.

525 TRESPASS

An image of illicitly venturing into another's house or onto their land may represent a desire to explore uncharted areas of sexual, spiritual or intellectual experience. A fear of being caught may represent your inhibitions about going on such a quest, but it might well be tinged with a frisson of excitement at the prospect of adventure (although, less positively, a trespass-dream may express a desire to commit adultery).

526 DESERTER

SEE ALSO
524: **Thief or robber** p.207,
Brother or sister p.93; 527:
Money p.199

Military personnel who desert their post present an ambiguous dream-image. If you are the deserter, you may be feeling guilty at your inability to confront a pressing emotional or psychological issue: the dream represents an attempt to escape – flight rather than fight. On the other hand, you may be demonstrating considerable courage in abandoning a hostile environment that you have endured for too long, or a lost or unfulfilling cause that has been sapping your energies for too little reward. If you are the one being left at your post by another, the dream could be prompted by a sense of parental neglect, by a feeling of being excluded from some group or activity, or by a bereavement or the break-up of a relationship. On the other hand, it could mark the beginnings of personal independence.

527 FORGERY

Unlike Freud, who viewed money as a symbol of excrement, recalling the English saying "where there's muck there's brass [money]", Jung saw money as an emblem of the power to achieve personal goals. Trying to spend counterfeit bills or banknotes may suggest that the dreamer feels tempted to take short cuts in pursuing those ambitions, indicating a general sense of weariness or frustration with the progress of self-development. Passing off fake money to someone close to you, or cheating them in some other way, may suggest your unwillingness to reveal your true self to that person.

528 COUNTERFEITER

If someone you know appears in a dream as a counterfeiter trying to press fake goods onto you, the image may be prompted by a suspicion that that person may not be acting with complete honesty in your professional, personal or spiritual life. The dream may alert us to the danger of too readily accepting promises that may turn out to be false.

529 SMUGGLING

Smuggling valuable but illicit goods may express the dreamer's wish to give friends the benefit of valuable new insights. Smuggling is not a selfless gift, however: the dreamer is counting on the gratitude of others. Another interpretation might see the smuggled goods as our true self – something we may be reluctant to reveal to others for fear of disapproval.

530 POISON

Just as vaccines, derived from disease-causing germs, protect us from disease, so a dream-poison may do good rather than harm. Dreamers may take poison to eliminate an emotion that is "poisoning" their exis-

> **SEE ALSO**
> 530: **Murder**
> p.182

tence – such as jealousy of a rival or obsession with a departed lover. However, a dream of administering poison to someone we know may reflect a genuine, though not necessarily murderous, hostility toward that person.

ENVIRONMENTS

AT HOME

531 COOKING

The cooking fire is traditionally the focus of the household (indeed, "focus" is Latin for "hearth") and thus can symbolize the deepest centre of our being. As a symbol of togetherness, preparing a meal can suggest a quest for love and affection.

532 FRYING

Frying is cooking with the constant risk of getting burned. As a symbol of sacrifice or death, the smoke can indicate a threat to the dreamer's aspirations. The dream may also be a salutary warning that if we avoid a problem we may make things worse for ourselves.

SEE ALSO
531: **Kitchen** p.241;
533, 534: **Ashes or dust** p.55, **Fire** p.285;
537: **Horn of Plenty** p.49, **Holy Grail** p.358

533 CINDERS

Cinders represent death or destruction, but with a subtle distinction from the more absolute death-symbol of ashes. Their glow may be a reminder of the life-force that characterized the deceased, or may also recall the inspiration we derived from a past endeavour.

The **grate (534)** swept clean may symbolize not only the burial-place of ruined ambitions, but also the cradle for projects as yet unborn.

535 KETTLE
The kettle with its spout is a symbol of male sexuality, carrying with it a suggestion that someone could be hurt unless boiling passions are handled carefully.

536 POTS AND PANS
These are also sexual symbols, female or male depending on whether the pot or its handle appears more prominently. The association with cooking may relate to some sexual matter bubbling away inside us, or to issues surrounding domestic arrangements with our partner.

537 CUP
When a cup is seen to symbolize female sexuality, drinking out of it indulges an erotic dream-wish. If it is hurled across a room by a man, it may express his anger with a woman or fear of female sexuality; if by a woman, the dream suggest an intention to use sex as a weapon. For Jungians, a cup may be a domesticated symbol for the abundance of life's opportunities, or the self-realization promised by the Holy Grail.

538 CUTLERY
Viewed collectively, knives, forks and spoons may suggest a desire for domestic security. The individual components take on a separate

symbolism. As scaled down, domesticated versions of weapons, a dinner knife and fork may suggest tamed aggression. Spoons have a female symbolism similar to cups, but if things are getting on top of us they may express a desire to be "spoon-fed" in life. A teaspoon could be telling us to take something in small steps or doses. A silver spoon might refer to someone we envy, as in the phrase "born with a silver spoon in the mouth."

539 WASHING THE DISHES

Doing the dishes may suggest a desire to wash away a feeling of shame or disgust, perhaps in connection with a sexual experience. Like washing hands, the dream may also denote a wish to deny responsibility.

540 HOUSEHOLD BREAKAGES

These may represent self-perceived character defects or flawed ideas. A cracked cup will often symbolize a lost love. A dream of breaking things around the house may express anger, disillusion or despair with whatever is symbolized by the household item, which will often have a sexual symbolism. A **broken window (541)**, which to Freud concerns female sexuality, may suggest to Jungians disillusionment with the world.

542 CLEANER

A cleaner evokes a range of symbolic associations. A woman in this unglamorous but essential role may recall your own hard-working mother. The house she is cleaning may symbolize the dreamer's self, suggesting a need to sort out neglected corners of our personality.

543 BROOM

The broom may represent, in its action of sweeping clean, the dreamer's urge to eliminate old ideas or habits, in order to prepare for a fresh approach. As a symbol of purification, the broom may indicate an authoritarian intolerance of views that perhaps complicate but also enrich a debate, either within oneself or in society at large.

544 VACUUM-CLEANING

Compared to sweeping up, there is something definitive and comprehensive about using a vacuum cleaner that suggests a desire to do away once and for all with every trace of a past action. Vacuuming dust may signify a wish to move on from the loss of someone who has left our lives.

SEE ALSO

539: **Hands** p.70; 540: **Drinking glass** p.256; 541, 543: **Halloween** p.158

545 WINDOW-CLEANING

Cleaning windows suggest that we are trying to get a clearer view of the world around us. We may feel that our perception has been blurred by our own excessive introversion.

546 WASHING MACHINE

Washing machine dreams frequently pitch us in the swirling water. As a womb-symbol, the water may point to deep-seated childhood issues that perhaps need to "come out in the wash". If water is accepted as an image of the unconscious, the turbulence of the wash may suggest it is time to confront old issues that are upsetting our peace of mind.

Clothes often symbolize the nudity they are meant to conceal, so the image of **washing or laundry hanging on a line (547)** may express a yearning for the lost innocence of childhood or a desire for self-exhibition and uninhibited sexuality.

548 SCULLERY

If a house is understood as a symbol of the self, the room used for the storage of kitchen utensils and doing messy kitchen work could be a symbol of the inner workings of the dreamer's mind – the storehouse of the unconscious.

SEE ALSO
545: **Windows** p.246;
547: **Nakedness** p.73; 548:
Cooking p.218,
Kitchen p.241

549 VARNISH

Applying a coat of varnish can suggest a wish to disguise your own self-perceived flaws, or to protect your beliefs from the criticism of others. It can also indicate a desire to gloss over problems in a relationship.

550 COLANDER OR SIEVE

A colander or sieve may be seen as standing for the process of developing a renewed outlook on life and "sifting out" or "rinsing away" unhelpful attitudes and ideas.

551 WHITEWASH

Whitewash may evoke its figurative sense as a cover-up for embarrassing misdeeds. This may relate to your own feelings of guilt, or your suspicion that others are concealing their real intentions.

OCCUPATIONS

552 ENGINEER

We may see the engineer as a redeemer, fixing the cogs and wheels of our world in times of trouble. Working in a basement – in the depths of our unconscious – he may prevent destructive urges from disrupting our conscious life. He may be a friend, relative or trusted adviser.

553 BAKER

The work of a baker has unmistakable associations with sexual intercourse, wholesome and healthy as bread itself. Loaves are strong images of male sexuality and the oven is an equally powerful symbol of the female. Baking itself may connote the gestation of pregnancy.

554 DENTIST

Not surprisingly, toothache stimulates dentist dreams. However, Jung noted that women's dreams with a dental stimulus are frequently associated with giving birth, turning the dentist, so to speak, into a symbolic obstetrician. Men's dreams of **tooth extraction (555)** are related by Freud to castration-fears, identifying the dentist with a parent.

556 BUILDER

As the (usually male) person working on the construction of a house, which often symbolizes the dreamer's self, the builder becomes a father-figure. Standing by partly completed walls, the builder may remind us of our childhood dependency. The dream may also express our resentment that our development continues to be influenced by our most authoritative role model.

557 POLICE OFFICER

Despite social change, this key authority figure is still most often perceived as male. Stern and unyielding or friendly and helpful, the police officer's manner may convey the image we have of our father. If he is arresting us, we may express resentment at being held back by an authoritarian father. A **policewoman (558)** can bring to mind a domineering mother or may suggest preoccupations with a woman being the dominant partner in a sexual relationship.

559 CONDUCTOR

Standing before a symphony orchestra, we may wish to control our own creative expression; we may also possess a perhaps unreasonable urge to shape the destiny of others. Music's frequent heavenly symbolism may also suggest a yearning for spiritual direction.

560 ADMIRAL

Given the phallic symbolism of ships, dreamers identifying with an admiral may feel the need to impose their will in a sexual relationship. Decked out in the full regalia of their rank, they may also be seeking the admiration of their partner.

561 BUTCHER

The butcher often appears in dreams with hands and apron covered in blood. Rather than signifying an act of violence, the blood might suggest that the dreamer has made some sacrifice in their personal

SEE ALSO
559: **Concert**
p.164

or professional life. Blood may also be associated with menstruation and indicate a fear of female sexuality.

562 CHEMIST

This may be interpreted as a symbolic reference to alchemy, which Jung relates to the dreamer's process of inner transformation. Dreamers identifying themselves with a chemist may be trying to concoct a formula for self-fulfilment.

563 MECHANIC

The mechanic is often seen floundering around dismantled machinery he cannot reassemble. We may recognize in him our own distress with the task of imposing order on the chaos of our waking life.

SEE ALSO
563: **Engineer** p.225; 565: **Hero** p.85; 573: **Dentist** p.226, **Builder** p.226, **Engineer** p.225, **House** p.237

564 MINER

Working in the bowels of the earth, the miner is digging deep into the dreamer's unconscious to find the ore that may yield precious insights. The miner may be seen hauling his load to the surface, the conscious mind, where the dreamer must transform the nuggets into real wisdom.

565 SOLDIER

A soldier often represents a hero fighting for a just cause. As symbol of the Jungian archetypal Hero (see p.16), the soldier becomes a role model inspiring dreamers in their personal struggles to succeed in life. If the phallic symbol of the soldier's weapon appears prominently, Freudians might see the dream as expressing a sexual urge.

566 SAILOR

As adventurers, sailors are likely to express the more daring aspects of the dreamer's character. Their element being the sea, a common Jungian symbol of the unconscious, the dream may evoke a wish to venture into hitherto unexplored areas of the inner self.

567 PLUMBER

The pipes and valves of a house's plumbing may be the symbols of either our body organs or our inner mental or emotional workings. In the context of pregnancy, the plumber may stand for the doctor, obstetrician or gynaecologist. The care or clumsiness with which he goes about the task may correspond to the confidence or anxiety we feel about having an internal examination. Seeing oneself in the role of the plumber may indicate a process of self-examination, exploring one's inner self and seeking to carry out repairs.

568 DOCTOR

A physician is a classic parent-figure, so if the dreamer is the patient they may experience what psychoanalysis calls transference, redirecting toward the doctor the childhood feelings they had, and perhaps continue to have, for their mother or father. These may be revealed by emotions that the doctor evokes in the dream – sexual desire, fear or hatred.

569 NURSE

The dream image of a nurse is unequivocally maternal. Dreamers may see themselves as a nurse, perhaps expressing a wish to be a mother, or as a patient wishing to be mothered. A domineering senior nurse, often called a "sister", may evoke childhood rivalry with a female sibling.

570 WAITER OR WAITRESS

SEE ALSO
568: **Father**
p.92; 569:
Mother p.92

Dreamers may see themselves in the role of a waiter or waitress in a restaurant and the quality of the service they provide may express concern about their relationship to people outside their family circle: obsequious or considerate, efficient or clumsy, polite or over-familiar.

571 SECRETARY

Dreamers can feel ambivalent about whether the boss or the secretary is playing the dependent role. A woman secretary shielding an executive from unwelcome callers may be a protective mother-figure. A secretary in traditional subservient role may suggest, in the male or female dreamer, desires for sexual domination.

572 OFFICIAL

The "faceless" bureaucrat may express our own lack of emotion or a frustration with the coldness we feel exists among friends and family. Bureaucrats may symbolize the machinery of a world that resists our efforts to succeed with work or personal creativity.

BUILDINGS

SEE ALSO

572: **Bureau-cracy, Stacks of paper** p.35;

573: **Fire** p.285;

574: **Defendant in court** p.37,

Trial p.208,

Lawyer p.209,

Jury p.211,

Verdict p.211

573 BUILDING

Dream-buildings often represent different aspects of the self, perhaps indicating the dreamer's concern about some weakness or failing. However, a building on fire, although an image of destruction, may have a positive meaning. As a symbol of liberation, a building-fire could urge dreamers to eliminate dead wood blocking new paths to progress.

574 LAW COURT

The law court may focus on the dreamer's capacities for judgment in complicated conflicts among work colleagues, friends or members of the family.

575 PALACE

A palace may represent your aspirations to a different lifestyle, or else a warning against adopting a pretentious façade. If a royal figure appears, he or she may represent nostalgia for the security of the family.

576 LIBRARY

A library usually stands for the world of ideas and knowledge. Books on a shelf out of reach may represent ideas beyond the dreamer's present understanding of life. Being distracted by another reader may suggest, beyond a failure to concentrate, the possibility that the ideas being considered are not worth our attention.

577 WINDMILL

As a grinder of flour for bread, the windmill may represent our deepest springs of creativity. Or a dreamer might identify with a windmill if he or she is the family's breadwinner.

578 LIGHTHOUSE OR BEACON

A lighthouse may appear as a beacon guiding dreamers through a dense fog of confusing ideas. When interpreting such a dream, bear in mind that the lighthouse indicates an area to avoid, not the direction in which you should be heading. Dreamers must rely on their own resources (for example, intelligence or flexibility) to avoid foundering. For Freud, of course, a lighthouse is an unequivocal phallic symbol rising beside the maternal image of the ocean.

579 EIFFEL TOWER

The French capital city of Paris has associations with revolutionary passions and romantic elegance. Its most prominent and famous landmark, the Eiffel Tower, presents a powerful erotic symbolism, a heady image of male sexuality.

580 CLOCK TOWER

A clock tower, such as the one known as "Big Ben" alongside London's Houses of Parliament, could be a grand symbol of an encounter with destiny. Ticking clocks commonly represent the heart and the passage of life. The clock tower combines this with the phallic form to offer an image of male courage and emotional development. Evoking great occasions, the sonorous chimes of Big Ben – or indeed the striking of a clock in a church tower – may relate to a momentous personal event, such as marriage or new job.

581 FACTORY

A factory may represent your creative work, viewed from the aspect of hard toil. A factory on strike may suggest an obstacle to creativity, such as writer's block. An endless production line most obviously suggests frustration with our career or relationships.

582 GASWORKS

The smell of gas may threaten to become sulphurous in a dream, making the gasworks a possible image

SEE ALSO

577: **Bread** p.144; 580: **Parliaments** p.36; **Churches** p.49; **Clocks** p.249

of hell. On the psychological plane, hell in turn is a symbol of the unconscious, and the dream may suggest a distaste for confronting the darker sides of our personality.

583 WATERWORKS

A dream of waterworks can conjure up the associations of water with the womb, turning the whole dream-edifice into a gigantic and perhaps daunting representation of the dreamer's mother.

584 PUBLIC HOUSE OR BAR

The bar or pub presents an arena in which dreamers can overcome their inhibitions. A convivial atmosphere at the bar may emphasize a wish to break with feelings of isolation. But involvement in a brawl could signify repressed emotions boiling over into dangerous, uncontrolled anger. Drunkenness can also suggest a loss of control, or a desire to obliterate uncomfortable emotions rather than confront them. On the other hand, a pleasant feeling of merriment might suggest that you have absorbed intoxicating insights and are prepared to face the future with optimism.

SEE ALSO
583: **Plumber** p.229; **Water** p.284; 588: **Windows** p.246

An **inn (585)** is like a pub, but with the difference that it offers a place to sleep overnight. It may be envisioned as having a more tranquil atmosphere than a pub, especially if it has a rural setting, suggesting the dreamer's desire for a secure environment in which to deal with the repressed impulses in the unconscious.

586 FARM

In the rustic setting of a farm, the dreamer may be yearning for a simpler, more down-to-earth approach to life. As a sign of just what such a life might entail, manure in the farmyard may point to financial and other obstacles to the realization of the dream.

587 HOUSE

A symbol of the self, the house often more specifically represents the body. An abandoned house in disrepair may indicate the dreamer's neglect of physical or emotional health. At a mental level, a house all shuttered up can suggest that we are blind to what is going on in the outside world.

Dreams of an **unfinished house (588)** can be a motivation for redoubled effort rather than a cause for despair. Only the smug imagine the self as anything but unfinished. A half-built house suggests what we need – maybe more windows on the outside world or better access to unconscious impulses in the basement.

589 DOORS

While Freud and Jung agreed that a house may symbolize the body, they differed about the house's doors. For Freud, doors are dream-images of a body's orifices. For Jung, doors express the dreamer's relationship to their inner and outer worlds. A door opening outward, according to the Jungian view, suggests the dreamer's need to open up to others. Opening inward, the door could mean a wish to explore the inner self.

590 WALLS

Walls may offer protection but may also imprison us in our fears. We can find brief comfort behind walls that keep out the forces of change, but one day we will have to venture outside to face reality.

591 CEILING

In modern parlance, the term "glass ceiling" means the limits imposed on a person's professional advancement, especially for women (or ethnic minorities), who may dream of banging their heads on this obstacle to higher aspirations.

592 FLOORS

From a Jungian perspective, the floors or stories of a house represent our unconscious, consciousness and higher spiritual aspirations. Rickety stairs and bolted doors to the basement or attic may symbolize the difficulties of penetrating the unconscious or progressing to a higher mental plane.

Riding impassively on an **escalator (593)** between floors may express the unemotional role dreamers play in their sexual relations, given the phallic symbolism that Freud attributes to stairs. According to the Jungian idea that stairs represent psychological growth, a dream of walking against the direction of the escalator suggests a frustration at the lack of personal progress.

594 LIVING ROOM

In the Jungian scheme, the rooms of a house symbolize compartments of the self. The living room is the realm of our conscious mind, the part of ourselves that we are happiest to reveal to others.

595 FURNITURE

Furniture may symbolize our thoughts and feelings. Cleaning and rearranging it may put more order in

SEE ALSO
590: **Prison** p.112; 592: **Attic or garret** p.242, **Basement** p.245; 593: **Steps and stairs** p.116, **Elevator** p116

our lives. Finding furniture broken or in disarray may express a time of emotional crisis and disruption in our home life or work.

An **unfurnished house (596)** may suggest a bleak self devoid of feeling or thought. More positively, the empty house may indicate a place of new opportunities, ready to be furnished with fresh experiences.

597 WARDROBE OR DRESSING ROOM

Storing clothes (exterior symbols of the inner self), the wardrobe or dressing room may express the personal image dreamers want to present to the outside world – or Jungian terms, the archetypal Persona (see p.16). If a wardrobe overflowing with clothes suggests extravagance or even exhibitionism, a locked wardrobe indicates that the dreamer is intent on hiding from public scrutiny.

598 KITCHEN

The kitchen generally conjures up images of love and affection associated with the domestic hearth and the preparation of food and drink for others. Male and female sexuality are abundantly symbolized in the room's utensils and vessels. Something burning in the kitchen should alert dreamers to a problem in their family life.

SEE ALSO
598: **Cooking,
Frying** p.218,
Scullery
p.223

599 BEDROOM

The bedroom is associated with sleep, birth and sex. For a dreamer, the bedroom can also be seen as a last resting place. Parents sleeping there may evoke images – or memories – of their death. An empty bedroom may symbolize the dreamer's own death.

600 BATHROOM

Seen relaxing in a warm tub in the bathroom, dreamers may imagine themselves back in the mother's womb. A window letting cool air into the bathroom can be a reminder that the dreamer's place is out there in the real world.

601 ATTIC OR GARRET

The happy jumble of the attic, symbol of our higher aspirations and creativity, may express the dreamer's welter of spiritual or creative ideas waiting to be put into some coherent form. An overly neat and tidy attic may suggest a too formal and timid approach to the spiritual life.

SEE ALSO
603: **Tunnel**
p.27; 605: **Walls**
p.238, **Prison**
p.112

We often keep a **trunk, chest or box (602)** up in the attic, where the contents may acquire a spiritual significance. The trunk could be seen as a storage place for projects the dreamer has set aside. The dream may be a reminder to retrieve those aspirations from the trunk rather than leave them to gather dust. For long-harboured ambitions, a trunk can be a treasure-trove, suggesting fulfilment – or it might resemble a coffin, indicating that it may be time to let go of unrealistic goals.

603 CHIMNEY
The chimney is traditionally the passage leading from the fires of hell, the route taken by witches on the way to their Sabbath. The imagery is laden with sexuality, male or female, depending on whether the chimney is viewed from outside or inside. A dreamer inside a chimney may be feeling claustrophobic, either literally or metaphorically.

604 GARDEN GATE
For a dreamer who is feeling too much absorbed by office work or city life, a garden gate may represent a welcome invitation to a more natural environment.

605 FENCE
Some dreamers may see in a fence a protection against the unwelcome curiosity of strangers. However, a fence may be a warning against excessive introversion, shutting yourself off from contact with the enriching ideas of the outside world.

606 GREENHOUSE OR CONSERVATORY

A conservatory or hothouse full of exotic plants projects an image of the unconscious that keeps the dreamer's unacknowledged instincts under glass and under control. The dreamer may want a peep at a tropical wilderness but without risking the dangers of a real jungle.

607 FOUNTAIN

The fountain has a rich mythological symbolism as the source of life, eternal youth and knowledge. A dreamer may regard a fountain as a symbol of encourage-ment and renewed hope after a period of depression or bereavement. A dream-fountain

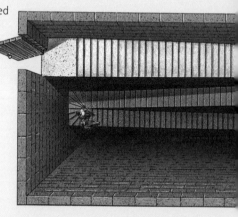

SEE ALSO
606: **Jungle**
p.299; 607:
Water p.284

could suggest the release of new creativity in an artist who feared that his or her inspiration had dried up. As the source of life, the fountain may stand for the dreamer's mother.

608 BASEMENT

The basement symbolizes the unconscious, where we go to explore urges and impulses that are trying to work their way into the consciousness. A **cellar (609)** shares the symbolism of the unconscious, but as a store-room for wine or food it may evoke instincts of a more explicitly carnal nature.

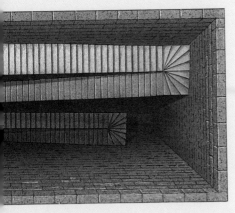

610 GARAGE

Traditionally a masculine preserve in our waking life, the garage as a shelter for the car is a dream-symbol of feminine sexuality. A dreamer who is fixing the car may be dealing with sexual problems in a relationship.

611 WINDOWS

Like doors, windows are female sexual symbols for Freudian interpreters. For Jung, windows offer a view of the outside world. Opening a window may represent a willingness to let in new ideas. Looking in at someone else's window may be the act of someone who is overly interested in the lives and ideas of others – perhaps to the point of voyeurism – instead of examining their own.

612 DRAPE OR CURTAIN

A drape or curtain may express a wish to be invisible and retreat from the outside world, or it may, through appearing to focus on modesty, in fact indicate the exact opposite: the dreamer's exhibitionist desire to go naked.

613 BALCONY

The balcony is a classic Freudian symbol for a woman's breasts – in colloquial French, *balcon* means precisely that and *balconnet* is a bra. Dreamers standing on a balcony are perhaps wishing to return to their mother's bosom. A male dreamer waving from the maternal balcony may, in Freudian terms, be flaunting his privileged position in Oedipal rivalry with his father.

614 CASTLE

A form of house, and as such representing the dreamer, a castle can be a fortress, a palace or a prison, and quite commonly all three. The apparent security that we may feel within our thick protective outer walls may be at the expense of emotional maturity and rewarding relationships with others.

A **ruined castle (615)** represents both destruction and the past. Its appearance may be a sign that we are ready to abandon outmoded patterns of thought and face the world with a new self-reliance.

616 STABLE

The stable is a haven of security. As the place where we keep a horse, which for Freud can symbolize the intimidating side of the dreamer's father, the stable allows us to contain our anxieties about our father. A stable may also suggest repressed sexuality, since horse-riding is a Freudian symbol of sex. For Jung, the horse represents humankind's harnessing of natural forces, making the stable a place where the dreamer can face those forces with confidence.

SEE ALSO
611: **Doors** p.238; 613: **Prison** p.112, **Palace** p.233, **House** p.237; 616: **Riding** p.134, **Horse** p.327

617 TOWER

A tower is a Freudian phallic symbol, signifying in its sturdiness or otherwise the sexual self-confidence of a male dreamer. As a place that may also represent our desire to shut ourselves away above the world and its concerns, it may be a form of isolating self-imprisonment in

our own anxieties. Fortified and seemingly impregnable, a tower may represent an imposing but perhaps emotionally impregnable figure in the dreamer's life, especially our father. A place where young women are imprisoned by tyrannical men in folk tales, a tower may symbolize for a female dreamer the oppressive influence of an authoritarian father, or of male authority in general.

618 VAULT

In its architectural sense of an arched ceiling, the vault often appears in churches and temples with painted stars and planets in imitation of "the vault of the heavens". As such it may evoke one's elevated spiritual thoughts. A vault may also recall a crypt or burial chamber, in which case it may represent intimations of death.

OBJECTS

619 CUSHIONS

Cushions may represent the reassuring presence of a loved one who makes life more comfortable and protects us from life's hard knocks. But shielding us from harsh realities might not always be the most helpful approach to adopt.

620 LAMP

The lamp is a symbol of life, knowledge and enlightenment. Casting a bright light, it may present an optimistic image of the dreamer's well-being and future prospects. A flickering lamp conveys fragility and uncertainty. A lamp unlit may be a symbol of death or ignorance.

621 AND 622 TIMEPIECES

Clocks (621) and **watches (622)** may appear as symbols of the heart and of the emotions. They evoke, too, the transience of human life. A stopped timepiece may focus on the dreamer's frozen emotions, perhaps at a time of bereavement or separation. A clock whose hands race out of control may indicate our feelings running amok.

SEE ALSO
617: **Lighthouse or beacon** p.234, **Eiffel Tower** p.234, **Castle** p.247; 618: **Churches** p.49; 620: **Candle** p.48, **Being of light** p.60; 621: **Clock tower** p.235

623 GARBAGE CAN/DUSTBIN

The trash that we discard in a garbage-can or dustbin may symbolize tiresome obligations, unpleasant memories or negative aspects of the personality that we would like to be rid of. A dream of throwing away what we consider to be trash may suggest an effort to evade responsibility or, on the other hand, a constructive desire to make a fresh start.

624 BASKET

Frequently associated with fruit, a basket may evoke an image of fertility and exuberant female sexuality. Depending on the basket's contents, the dream's eroticism may express youthful energy or ripe maturity.

625 BAG

A bag may symbolically carry the dreamer's hopes for the future. A heavy bag may suggest more projects than we can handle. An empty bag, however, far from meaning that we have no hopes, may express a wish to go out in search of new ideas, new goals.

626 CARPET

A carpet with a distinct floral design may be a symbol of a garden, evoking the Garden of Eden – especially if we can imagine it with a Tree of Life or Tree of Knowledge woven into its pattern. If a house represents the self, a carpet may be covering up access to a lower floor – perhaps the dreamer is attempting to deny impulses from the unconscious. The precise significance of the image may depend on the prominent hues and shapes in its design.

627 DISH

In dreams, a dish usually presents freshly cooked food served up to be eaten now – ideas to be tackled immediately. A dish of leftovers evokes old ideas that are to be assigned to the trash.

628 TICKET

A ticket expresses opportunity. The dream-image may conjure up a range of wishes associated with travel, winning a lottery or indulging the fantasies of a film or play. Dreamers searching for a ticket may be feeling anxiety about losing a chance of exploring new possibilities in their emotional or professional life.

SEE ALSO
624, 626:
Garden of
Eden p.32; 626:
Garden p.295,
Tree p.296

629 CAMERA

At a time when too many things are happening too fast, the camera may give dreamers the possibility of preserving an important event in their lives. A dream of using the camera to take a portrait may indicate a need to hold on to a person who is threatening to depart.

630 BOOKS

Books are symbols of wisdom and knowledge. Books that seem unintelligible can suggest that the dreamer is unable to concentrate on the tasks at hand or is losing all interest in the world of ideas.

631 PAPER

A blank sheet of paper may be a symbol of either hope or despair. The paper may represent an opportunity to create fresh ideas or the withering impression that you have none. Paper crumpled up or torn into pieces can signify the collapse of a cherished project or the rejection of outdated ideas.

SEE ALSO
630: **Library**
p.233; 632:
**E-mail error
message** p.38

632 COMPUTER

The computer may have replaced the typewriter, but the keyboard remains a Freudian symbol of female sexuality, as do the slots for disks, CD-ROMs and DVDs. Jungians focus on the screen as a projection of humankind's knowledge dispatched through cyberspace. Computer hackers correspond to Jung's Trickster archetype (see p.15) wreaking havoc in an orderly society.

633 RADIO

With voices evoking different images for each listener, the radio is a powerful medium of the individual imagination. A dream-radio may become the expression of a dreamer's inner voice. Receiving static instead of a clear signal suggests an inability to make contact with one's innermost thoughts.

634 TELEVISION

Television's role in our dreams is very much that of its cliché as a "window on the world". Dreamers imagining themselves on TV may seek to communicate emotions and ideas they feel unable to convey in waking life. The image may also arise from vanity or a craving for fame, or perhaps simply a desire for more attention from a loved one.

635 PERSONAL STEREO

Perhaps expressing a wish to concentrate on your own inner voice and shut out the unwelcome cacophony of the outside world, a dream of wearing a personal stereo may also warn against excessive introversion and avoidance of interaction with other people.

636 KNOT

Symbolizing the various ties formed in a lifetime, relationships with others, and also the interrelationship of ideas, the knot presents a view of the dreamer's life in all its complexity. A knot undone may be a symbol of death. To carefully untie a difficult knot expresses a readiness to deal with the intricacies of a problem rather than ignore them by impatiently cutting the knot in two. The knot also has erotic symbolism, the nuptial knot representing the married couple's personal and sexual union.

637 FAN

A charming image of female sexuality, a fan may appear to cool the dreamer's ardour. More often, the image is fanning the flames of the dreamer's passion.

638 WHEELBARROW

A wheelbarrow represents progress and the clearing of unwanted growth, but it is a vehicle that cannot move unless we push it, hence its other associations with energy and action. Filled with sundry household objects, it may suggest that you are making a determined break with the past.

SEE ALSO
638: **Wheel**
p.130

639 SEASHELLS

Both by its shape and its mythic link to Venus rising from the sea, famil-iar from Botticelli's painting, the shell represents female sexuality. From its association with the sea, it may also represent the unconscious and the dreamer's imagination.

640 CHAIR

The chair is an image of female sexuality, and the degree of comfort the chair offers can indicate how much at ease the dreamer feels with a female sexual partner. A broken chair or one that col-lapses under the dreamer's weight may signal the end of a sexual relationship.

641 SCISSORS

Scissors offer a graphic dream-image of sexuality, either male or female depending on whether they are closed or open.

642 DRINKING GLASS

Jungians often see the glass as an equivalent of the mythical Holy Grail, offering the dreamer spiritual love and wisdom. For Freudians, to dream of drinking from a glass expresses sexual desire, because, like other receptacles, the glass symbolizes the female genitals. A broken glass can represent broken virginity, a symbol explicitly enacted with the breaking of a wine glass at Jewish weddings.

643 HORSESHOE

As a good luck charm, the horseshoe may offer dreamers a promise of success, more specifically in their sexual life. A dream-game of pitching horseshoes at an iron peg makes this metaphor explicit.

644 NAILS

In Christian civilization, nails have long been associated with the Crucifixion. They may be symbols of persecution, punishment, torture, suffering and sacrifice, both for the dreamer and for others.

645 NUTS AND BOLTS

"Nuts and bolts" in the figurative sense draw our attention to the practicality of an undertaking rather than vague theoretical considerations or speculation. The objects also evoke female and male sexuality.

SEE ALSO
639: **Water** p.284; 640: **Flying in an incongruous vehicle** p.122; 642: **Cup** p.219, **Holy Grail** p.358; 644: **Jesus Christ** p.58, **Violence to the self** p.180

646 HAMMER

A hammer driving in a nail or metal stake may be seen as a symbol of willpower, the forceful energy that directs the dreamer's moral judgment. In ancient mythology, the hammer was a symbol of brute force, the instrument of gods of thunder and war, and may still evoke violence.

647 SCREWDRIVER

Beyond its primary phallic symbolism, the screwdriver may represent an instrument for putting the finishing touches to a project. The dream can express a determination to give work added security and stability.

648 MATCHES

Lighting a flame with matches could express the dreamer's desire for purification, enlightenment and spiritual love. Matches that fail to light can signal the frustrations of spiritual doubt. Dead matches may symbolize a faith extinguished.

SEE ALSO
646: **Nails** p.257; 648: **Flames** p.42; 649: **Cigar** p.48

649 CIGARETTE

A desire for oral sex may be expressed in the dream imagery of a cigarette, placed between the lips and cupped in the hands when being lit. A cigarette stubbed out may symbolize the end of a love affair.

650 PINS AND NEEDLES

Pins and needles present many images, all with a sexual symbolism – pricking a finger and drawing blood, threading the needle, and the action of sewing. The pleasure or pain evoked by the dream-image may convey desire or anxiety about the sexual act. A dream of pins and needles together may relate to the figurative sense of being in a state of nervous anticipation.

651 HAIRPIN

A hairpin may be a highly charged dream-image of female sexuality, both in its arched shape and in the classic seductive symbol of taking out a hairpin to undo a bun or chignon and release the hair.

652 PASSPORT

The passport may represent the dreamer's opportunity to escape from present frustrations. Opening the passport to find someone else's photograph may suggest that another person got the job – or the sexual partner – that the dreamer was coveting.

653 DRIVER'S LICENCE

A licence to drive symbolizes personal autonomy, placing us in charge of our own existence. Dreams of police confiscating the licence may indicate that someone who exerts a powerful influence in our life – not necessarily the authorities – is taking our destiny out of our hands.

654 SOAP

Mundane symbol of cleanliness, soap may express feelings of guilt that you want to wash away, or simply a need to put some order into your life. Dreamers who in childhood were threatened with having their mouths washed out with soap may see in the dream-image a warning about casual obscenity.

655 FLAG

The way in which a flag is treated may characterize the feelings that the dreamer has toward the country that the flag represents. Burned, torn or trampled underfoot, the flag may evoke either anger against the those who have attacked the flag or against the country itself. A sea of flags waving in a crowd may signify the dreamer's strong patriotic emotions, or equally strong foreboding about excessive nationalism.

Less literally, the flag as essentially a tribal emblem may stand for our entire network of family and friends. Are we at one with this personal "tribe"? Do we feel supported by it? Our positive or negative or neutral attitude to the dream-flag may reveal our unconscious feelings on these questions.

656 FLASHLIGHT OR TORCH

Dreamers may use a flashlight or torch to seek out truth and integrity in a world of ignorance and corruption, like the lantern which the ancient Greek statesman Demosthenes used in his futile attempt to find an honest man. A torch that flickers and goes out can represent sickness and death or the end of a once-brilliant hope or aspiration.

657 BABY CARRIAGE/PRAM

Dreamers who imagine themselves in a pram may be yearning to return to the secure and carefree life of a baby. Like other vehicles, the pram may also be a phallic symbol, perhaps pointing to sexual issues with their origins in childhood.

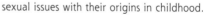

658 AND 659 UMBRELLA AND PARASOL

As a protection against the life-giving rain, an **umbrella (658)** may suggest the dreamer's timid refusal of physical or spiritual fertility. To shelter under an umbrella may be an undignified flight from reality and responsibility. In its sexual symbolism, the umbrella changes its gender when it is imagined opened (female) or closed (male).

Walking upright in the sun under a **parasol (659)**, the dreamer assumes the proud posture of someone with elevated aspirations. A white parasol with spokes like beams of light may symbolize the sun itself. The parasol-dream may represent a moment of creative inspiration.

660 PLASTIC FLOWERS

If flowers are a symbol of sexuality and spring blossom an image of innocence, then fake flowers may represent our mistrust of someone's professed intimate emotions.

EDUCATION

661 SCHOOL

As the symbol of youth and emotional immaturity, a school may evoke feelings of happiness or anxiety. A school unchanged since childhood may represent a nostalgic desire to rediscover youthful ideals. A

SEE ALSO
658: **Rain**
p.284; 659:
Summer's day
p.283

ruined or dilapidated school (662) can present the collapse of youthful illusions. The dream may emphasize a need not to dwell on the past – to move on.

663 TEACHER

A teacher is a dream-image of authority, feared or admired as a father-figure or mother-figure. He or she may be seen as having shaped our life for good or ill. A teacher may also represent within the dreamer's own personality a force to discipline disruptive urges in the unconscious.

664 INK

Ink, which so many of us still instinctively associate with our schooldays, usually appears in dreams spilled across a sheet of paper. The spilled ink may suggest that some dramatic fault has been committed. The shade of the ink can indicate the nature of the fault: black might symbolize an evil deed or some nocturnal act, red an act associated with blood – perhaps sexual rather than violent, but possibly both.

665 SCHOOL BAG

A dreamer bowed down by a cumbersome school bag is likely to feel equally weighed down by the past. On the other hand, when we open up a school bag full of books, papers, pens, sandwiches and apples, our accumulation of knowledge becomes a positive and happy experience.

666 NOTEBOOKS

Neatly kept school notebooks with immaculate columns of figures and vocabulary lists may evoke a

SEE ALSO
662: **Ruined city** p.281; 663: **Father** p.92; **Mother** p.92; 664: **COLOURS** pp.341–343; 665: **Quills or pens** p.47

desire to put a similar order into the dreamer's adult life. Exercises covered with scribbles may represent the dreamer's inner confusion, though a few flowers or planes drawn in the margins suggests that some minds might cope more creatively with disorder than with discipline.

667 CLASSROOM

The classroom is where we continue to feel judged by our peers and by an authority figure embodied by the teacher. Sitting at the back to avoid the teacher's eye may express a desire to dodge responsibility. Eagerly raising a hand in the front row, we may be yearning for attention and a chance to prove ourselves.

668 PLAYGROUND

The playground represents the world of recreation necessary to balance our time at work. Dreamers not joining in other children's games may reveal an emotional vacuum in their adult life. Reluctance to leave the playground to return to class may suggest a dislike of current work circumstances or a preference for sensual rather than intellectual pursuits.

669 BULLYING

In a bullying dream, people usually identify with the victim rather than the bully. Dreamers may be expressing old memories of school experiences, or the bully might represent an aggressive or domineering parent or partner. The dream may reveal an unconscious wish to dominate or be dominated, perhaps in a homosexual relationship, if both victim and bully are the same sex.

670 BLACKBOARD

The blackboard sets out in white on black – symbols of light and shadow – the ideas that guide the dreamer though life. The insights are set against a black background representing a constant reminder of the spiritual void on which humankind must make its imprint. But the impermanent **chalk (671)** is a reminder against having rigid ideas. Sometimes, effacing what is written prepares the way for new insights.

In Freudian terms, the stick of chalk may take the dreamer out of the spiritual world of the blackboard to the down-to-earth realm of male sexuality. Holding the chalk can evoke masturbation and breaking the chalk a fear of castration.

672 DESK

A classroom desk may represent your personal domain, your most private self. Marking out your territory by carving initials on the desktop, you may be expressing a need to reaffirm your identity to the

SEE ALSO
667: **Examinations** p.188;
669: **Domination** p.45

outside world. Rummaging inside the desk may symbolize sexual intercourse since, as a receptacle, the desk is also an image of female sexuality.

673 COLLEGE OR UNIVERSITY

Whether or not the dreamer actually attended college, it can represent an arena of higher intellectual or spiritual striving. Traditional university buildings with Gothic towers and ivy-covered walls may indicate respect for the learning process. A colder, more impersonal concrete establishment may suggest alienation.

A dream of a **graduation ceremony (674)** might indicate how we genuinely feel about our intellectual or spiritual progress. Are we one of those being praised and congratulated? Or are we at the back of the hall, an uncomfortable onlooker at the sight of others' success? A sign that we may not yet feel sufficiently clothed in wisdom is the dream-embarrassment of turning up either without our robes or completely naked.

675 PUNISHMENT IN CLASS

Dreams of punishment in class evoke submission to the teacher as a stern father-figure. Corporal punishment provoked by deliberate mischief can suggest

SEE ALSO
673: **Examinations** p.188;
675: **Sado-masochistic acts** p.45

the dreamer's wish for masochistic sexual pleasure. Milder punishment for bad schoolwork – being kept after school – may point to feelings of guilt about not meeting family or professional obligations.

676 SCHOOL BELL

A school bell often invades dreams in place of the alarm clock going off in the waking world. If the bell is announcing the termination of classes, dreamers might feel blessed relief that a trying period in their life is over. Coming at the end of a recreation break, the bell could evoke regret that a happy moment, perhaps an erotic experience, must also come to an end.

677 END OF SEMESTER/TERM

Our celebrations for the end of a period of hard work may be tinged with regret for the loss of stimulation and togetherness. However, the celebration can express joyful anticipation of the next stage in our personal development.

THE THEATRE AND THE CIRCUS

678 STAGE

As Shakespeare said: "All the world's a stage." A dream-stage places one world of illusions inside another, the world of our dreams. As such, the stage expresses our efforts to understand appearances. If we see ourselves on stage we may be preoccupied with how we appear to others – and to ourselves – in the waking world.

679 STAGE PLAY

A dream-play often reveals the thoughts and feelings that the dreamer is least capable of accepting or

> **SEE ALSO**
> 678: **Wearing a mask** p.23

confronting. Our unconscious may employ the action of a dream-play to express our most extreme and unpalatable emotions, which in our waking hours we may forcibly exclude from the conscious mind. We are thus alerted to powerful emotions represented by the perhaps melodramatic twists and turns of the drama unfolding on stage before us. Do we see our life as basically a comedy, a tragedy, a farce, a fantasy or, more likely, a combination of all these elements?

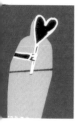

680 ACTOR OR ACTRESS

The actor or actress may appear as an expression of the dreamer's chosen public image, in the Jungian sense of the archetypal Persona (see p.16). A particular character in a play may embody the dreamer's highest aspirations or lower impulses. Boos or applause may reveal how well – which may also mean how hypocritically – the character has disguised the dreamer's real nature. A star whom you greatly admire may represent your mother or father, or your yearning for glamour.

681 COMEDIANS

Comedians are a toned-down version of Jung's archetypal Trickster (see p.15). Not usually quite so savage and outrageous in their rebellion against society, comedians nonetheless do make fun of established authority and perhaps also mock the dreamer's own vanity. The dreamer may have an envious wish to share some of the comedian's rebellious nature.

682 MOVIE ACTING

A dreamer acting in a film may be seeking to add a veneer of glamour to the expression of unconscious urges – homicidal, adulterous, felonious, incestuous – about which he or she may feel ashamed. A dream of film acting suggests a desire to distance yourself from what is portrayed on the screen and may at the same time be a warning against denying responsibility for important acts in waking life.

683 STUNT PERFORMER

People who stand in for the stars to perform stunts, such as spectacular acts of death-defying courage, are perhaps projections of your anxiety about excessive demands being made on you in your emotional or working life. Jumping from a train hurtling toward disaster, for example, could signify a fantasy escape from a sexual relationship. The feeling of being put-upon at work could be enhanced by the stunt-performer's typical anonymity – it is always the star, not the stunt man, who takes the credit.

SEE ALSO
680: **Wearing a mask** p.23,
Making a speech p.206,
Unruly audience p.206;
681: **Clowns** p.276

684 TV TALK SHOW

Perhaps symbolizing a craving for celebrity, a talk show may also indicate a belief that our opinions do not get the attention they deserve.

685 TV QUIZ GAME

Appearing on a TV quiz may be a symptom of low self-esteem or a frustration that our talents are not being justly rewarded. If there are big money prizes, the dream may also express financial anxieties.

686 CIRCUS

The ultimate theatre in the round, the great ring of the circus embraces the whole transient spectacle of our lives, ranging from courage and daring to comedy, animal passions and an ever-present fear of the unpredictable and death. An empty circus ring may express our feeling that life is passing us by – but it may also represent the expectant arena of exciting new possibilities.

687 CONJURORS AND MAGICIANS

Conjurors perform tricks as feats of illusion and sleight of hand. Winning admiration not for their mystic powers but for their human skills, the circus magician may impress on us the need to be wary of someone whose charisma might only be superficial.

688 FIRE-EATER

The performer spouting forth fire conjures up an image of expelling
inner rage. Ridding himself
of its destructive power, the
performer presents fire as a
controlled force, tamed and harmless.

689 JUGGLERS

The skill and tension of the juggler's act
may symbolize our own feelings of
having to "juggle" the various aspects
of our lives to keep abreast of our
many responsibilities.

690 CLOWNS

Clowns express an essential element of the archetypal Trickster (se
p.15) with a self-mockery that paro-
dies the foolishness and absurdity of
society's conventions – and perhaps
also the dreamer's own pretensions.

691 ACROBATS

Very often working in a male and female partnership, circus acrobats and tumblers symbolize an equal union of male and female strengths and grace, cemented by total trust. If the acrobats are you and your partner, your unconscious could be telling you that you have found your soul mate. If there is a slip and a fall, dream-acrobats are advising us that the harmony of our relationship may involve taking risks.

692 LION TAMER

In Jungian terms, tamed animals indicate the impressive results that people can achieve when working on their primitive urges. The lion tamer handles wildness with caresses and whispers of persuasion. The dream can point to the personal benefits of seeking to acknowledge and work with your baser instincts rather than trying to repress them by force. If you believe the lion might stand for someone you are close to, perhaps you desire unrealistically to restrain their true exuberance or passions. Or the tamer's whip may express sado-masochistic desires.

For Jungians, other performing animals at the circus, such as horses, elephants and **seals (693)** also represent a dreamer's base instincts. However,

SEE ALSO

688: **Fire** p.285; 692: **Sado-masochistic acts** p.45, **Whips** p.46, **Lion** p.320; 693: **The sea** p.284

Freudian interpreters see the training of animals to perform tricks for humans as fulfilling an unconscious wish for sexual domination.

694 RINGMASTER

Doing little apart from cracking his whip and bellowing commands at humans and animals, the ringmaster symbolizes the sterile, fear-based power of the tin-pot dictator. In dreams, he may be identified with your father or another male authority-figure in your life, or with someone who demands more emotionally than they give in return.

CITIES AND TOWNS

695 CITY

Dreamers may feel oppressed by the impersonal character of an endlessly sprawling city, with its long wide streets, tall buildings and dense traffic. Streets either totally empty or crowded with expressionless, hurrying people may emphasize a need for more intimacy. The city's vast size can be intimidating, forcing the dreamer into retreat, or acting as a challenge for the dreamer to make a personal impact.

SEE ALSO

694: **Domina-tion** p.45; 695, 696, 697: **House** p.237

696 TOWN

In contrast to a city, a dream-town often has a more human dimension. Dreamers may find warmth in the cafés and narrow streets with bright, welcoming shop windows. Freud sees in the town an all-embracing image of woman, inviting or forbidding according to whether the streets are brightly lit or dark and empty. For Jung, the image of a subterranean town evokes the dreamer's unconscious and an urge to explore links with the rest of humanity through archetypal scenarios.

For some dream interpreters, the dream city or town is a representation of the self, like a house but on a much larger scale. How we feel about being in this place can reflect our own sense of optimism and well-being or of dissatisfaction and fear.

697 AND 698 SLUMS AND WEALTHY DISTRICTS

A run-down **slum quarter (697)** with dirty streets and dilapidated houses may represent social relationships of which we are ashamed. On the other hand, it may also suggest that the dreamer is looking for greater challenges and more honest and direct human relationships – perhaps in the face of the disapproval of friends and family who are more concerned to keep up appearances. If the town or city is taken as a representation of the self, seeing ourselves residing in the slums may be in indicator of low self-esteem. Alternatively, our fascination to explore areas that most people might normally avoid may reveal a covert desire to confront and understand all the facets of our true selves.

Conversely, if we dream of living in an **affluent quarter or suburb (698)**, this may indicate our general optimistic feeling that we are getting what we deserve in life. However, the opposite may be the case if we are merely passing through, admiring the fine houses and immaculate gardens but aware that we do not belong. Such alienation may also serve as a reminder that there can be more to life than the pursuit of material achievement.

699 TOWN ON A HILL

The settlement on a hill is a Jungian image of wisdom, heaven and the home of the gods; in religious terms it is the stronghold of the righteous, the New Jerusalem, the Heavenly City. The town's elevated position may also express the pride we feel in our progress (spiritual or material) – and a reminder, perhaps, not to forget the humility that keeps our feet on the ground.

700 WALLED CITY

A walled city may signify a conservative wish to resist change and to keep out new ideas. The values that the dreamer may want to protect within the walls are perhaps not strong enough to withstand the questioning of others. Alternatively, the city wall may point to an unconscious desire for seclusion. Even the most selfless people occasionally need time to themselves to recharge the energy that they expend in serving others. Often, such devoted people are also the most reluctant to admit their needs.

701 RUINED CITY

A city lying in ruins may symbolize the dreamer's neglect of relationships. This dream-image can also

SEE ALSO
698: **House**
p.237; 700:
Walls p.238;
701: **Ruined
castle** p.247,
**Ruined or
dilapidated
school** p.264

evoke the erosion of early ideals and goals, which may need reconstructing if they are now to prove practicable. If the ruins are ancient rather than recent, we may be yearning for a never-to-be-recovered – and perhaps over-idealized – past.

702 VILLAGE

A village may evoke an intimate community with simple, traditional values and rich in human contact. This idea may be attractive to dreamers who have become disillusioned with the rushed pace and impersonal life of the big city.

ELEMENTS AND SEASONS

703 DAWN

The beginning of a new day can signal fresh hope for the dreamer. The image of sunrise may appear in a dream to herald a sense that the dreamer is at last recovering from a long period of illness or bereavement. Dawn-dreams may also indicate our realization that friends, colleagues or family are starting to listen to an important idea that we have been trying to communicate – or that we are catching the first glimpse of an exciting new insight.

704 DAYLIGHT

Dreams of the bright light of day streaming through a window are often full of optimism, expressing an attraction to clear thinking and energetic activity. A ray of sunlight may alert the dreamer to the important role being played in their lives by a particular face or object that is illuminated in an otherwise darkened room.

705 SUMMER'S DAY

The hot sun and blinding light of a summer's day may represent a spiritual or intellectual shock of enlightenment or a startling break with an old belief. The noonday sun may also be experienced as aggressive, perhaps reflecting the dreamer's resistance to ideas they feel are being arrogantly foisted upon them.

706 AIR

An element evoking freedom and the spirit, air makes its presence felt in dreams as a gentle breeze or the exhilarating sensation of floating. Air may express a feeling of self-confidence, an ability to think clearly and act decisively. A strong wind may relate to a time of upheaval in your life.

SEE ALSO

706: **Flying unaided** p.119, **Bathroom** p.242, **Storms** p.289, **Hurricane** p.289

707 WATER

A common symbol of creativity, water was associated by Freud with the womb. A dreamer floating happily in water may thus express a wish to be "back home" with their mother. For Jung, water is a major symbol of the unconscious in which dreamers may find a source of creative energy or explore the depths of their imagination. A dream of floundering in water can signal the careful groundwork needed to avoid sinking.

708 THE SEA

The sea is a symbol of female sexuality in the Freudian view, and tides express the ebb and flow of sexual union. To Jung, the sea represents the unconscious.

709 RAIN

A light rain may be bringing together the elements of water and air, imagination and freedom, to fertilize the dreamer's new project. On the other hand, a torrential downpour may indicate that the dreamer feels pessimistic at the prospect of carrying the project through to fruition.

710 FLOOD

Like its biblical antecedent, a flood may be seen as a preparation for new life, a fresh start. This meaning fits in with the Freudian symbolism of water as the womb, as well as Jung's concept of the Deluge as both deadly and life-giving. As a mother-image, a flood submerging a house, symbol of the self, could express an unconscious fantasy about incest with the mother. Or it may relate to a feeling that we are being overwhelmed by the pressures of school, work, family or relationships.

711 FIRE

Evoking powerful emotions such as envy, lust and passion, fire is an ambiguous symbol – it destroys, yet in doing so purifies and clears a path for new growth. It hints at the need to clear up troubling issues that have been cluttering a relationship – or perhaps to seek a fresh start. A house-fire may be symbolically eliminating precisely those factors that have perhaps prevented us from starting anew.

SEE ALSO
707, 708:
Drowning p.27,
Gushing water
p.48; 711:
Candle p.48,
Flames p.42

712 BURNT WOOD

Charred or burnt wood may symbolize a dreamer's dying passion for a loved one or waning enthusiasm for a once-important idea.

713 EARTH

This is a symbol of fertility and is often related to the feminine aspect of a personality. Soil on which nothing is growing must be dug up to receive the seeds of new life. Earth may also keep us in firm contact with reality, but we should be aware of becoming "stuck in the mud".

714 EARTHQUAKE

An earthquake may symbolize the eruption of pent-up sexual passions or, for Jungians, dark repressed forces in the unconscious that threaten to engulf and devastate the dreamer's conscious life. However, it may also suggest the liberation of creative energies.

SEE ALSO
712: **Ashes or dust** p.55; 713: **The Earth** p.374; 715, 716: **Blindness** p.100, **Fire** p.285

715 AND 716 FOG OR SMOKE

Fog or smoke may symbolize our groping toward the light of insight. If we sense that the light is about to break through, we may be left in a state of expectation rather than confusion.

717 SNOW

Snow may be a symbol of purification, but its white blanket may also be seen in dreams as covering up the complexities and rich diversity of life. Also, snow freezes the emotions and may be a symbolic reminder to dreamers of a need to show more warmth to people around them.

718 ICE

Ice is likely to signify emotional rigidity, an indifference to the feelings of others. The image may offer a warning against holding too steadfastly to a position that prevents the creative flow of the dreamer's own ideas and resists suggestions from others.

719 LIGHTNING

Lightning can suggest inspiration or a flash of brilliance that is impressive but short-lived. As the phenomenon that sparks fire on earth, lightning also has a sexual symbolism of sperm.

720 THUNDER

Thunder may signal a challenge which the dreamer may be awaiting with some anxiety. However, it may also symbolize the fearsome voice of the dreamer's father or some other authority-figure (in many cultures, thunder represents the voice of a powerful male deity, such as the Greek

Zeus or the Norse Thor – or God when giving the Ten Commandments). Another weather feature that is often coupled with a thunderstorm is **hail (721)**, which may appear as the pricks of conscience, perhaps as a reminder to the dreamer to complete a tiresome task.

722 DARKNESS

Darkness descending may suggest that repressive forces in the unconscious are preventing the dreamer from dealing with important but uncomfortable feelings or thoughts in the conscious mind.

723 STORMS

Storms may express the dreamer's own rage or perhaps evoke the anger, as with thunder, of a fierce authority-figure. The dream-storm may also conjure up the excitement of tumultuous passions which dreamers desire as a change from the banality of daily routine.

A **tropical storm or hurricane (724)** is often identified with a divine or exalted spirit which the dreamer may fear – or yearn – to confront. A hurricane or **tornado (725)** flattening houses or hurling vehicles through the air may signify the fragility of the material world or our own insecurity.

SEE ALSO
722: **Blindness** p.100; 723: **Air** p.283; 726: **Fog or smoke** p.286

726 CLOUD

The appearance of a cloud may suggest the obscuring of insight. The commonly depicted image of someone floating on a celestial cloud may express the dreamer's desire to make the idea of death more palatable.

727 TWILIGHT

Looking back on the day and forward to night, twilight is the time of blurred outlines, when things may not be as frightening as they seem.

728 BLUE SKY

Blue sky may conjure up spiritual aspirations, inklings of an infinite divinity. However, a blue sky that evokes happiness is unlikely to appear without a cloud here and there to remind dreamers that such happiness should be enjoyed while it lasts.

729 RAINBOW

For Jungians, a rainbow is a spiritual symbol of redemption, forgiveness

SEE ALSO

730: **Beach** p.153; 733: **Symbols of death** p.108

and promise, signifying the dreamer's quest for self-knowledge. The rainbow represents for the enlightened mind a bridge between heaven and earth. A dream-rainbow clearly arching from the earth to the skies and back down to earth may fill dreamers with optimism about the soaring possibilities of their earth-bound creativity.

730 SAND

The body sinking luxuriantly into warm sand can evoke a need for rest, security and regeneration, associated with a desire to return to the mother's womb, of which sand, like the sea, is a strong psychological symbol. Sand is a common dream-image of time passing – in an hourglass or slipping through the fingers. The notion of transience is emphasized in the image of a **sandcastle (731)** submerged by the sea.

732 AUTUMN LEAVES

In dreams, falling leaves are a classic symbol of melancholy and anxieties about death, just as damp leaves lying thick on the ground suggest decay. Bright red and yellow leaves may evoke the rejuvenation that is to follow the fall and winter.

733 HARVEST

A harvest may suggest that dreamers are expecting to reap the benefits from a period of intense activity. Harvest time may also evoke an image of death embodied by the Grim Reaper. In this sense the harvest also signals the start of a new life-cycle, prompting a search for fresh opportunities. Associated with the end of summer, **hay (734)** can symbolize a time of opportunity, relating to the notion of "making hay while the sun shines".

LANDSCAPES

735 COUNTRYSIDE

An idyllic sun-drenched landscape of meadows and trees and perhaps a babbling brook may express the stressed urban dreamer's wish for the good life. That same landscape in bad weather may be a warning that grim realities stand in the way of wish-fulfilment.

A **view or vista (736)** of the countryside, perhaps at a distance or through a window, accentuates the sometimes over-idealistic character of aspirations to a more natural existence.

737 HILLS

Hills may be viewed as the first manifestations of the earth's creation, rising from the vast undifferentiated plain at the beginning of time. Lacking the sublime challenge of mountains, hills afford a reassuring human dimension to the sacred and allow dreamers to contemplate self-understanding as a manageable task.

738 MOUNTAIN

A mountain, the contours or profile of which frequently resemble a woman's breast, represents for Freud an image of female sexuality. A dreamer looking up to the summit may be expressing anxiety about confronting that sexuality, just as standing on top looking down can signify a feeling of domination. For Jung, the mountaintop offers an elevated view

of the self; while looking at the peak from below could indicate the immensity of the challenge that the dreamer faces in grappling with all the facets of his or her personality.

739 FOREST OR WOOD

The darkness and dense concentration of trees and plants make of the forest an eloquent symbol of the unconscious and its concealed impulses. Jung sees in the fear of penetrating the forest the dreamer's anxiety about what the unconscious mind might reveal. For Freud, more literally, that penetration is a sexual act, the tangled vegetation a symbol of pubic hair.

740 ORCHARD

Like the fruit on its trees, an orchard may represent a dream of pregnancy. In an intellectual or spiritual domain, an orchard with unripe fruit may remind dreamers of how much work must be done to achieve their objectives. Fruit rotting in the grass may suggest that the dreamer is spoiling a chance of success by waiting too long to put ideas into action.

741 VINEYARD

The vineyard is the place where we can gather the fruit which, as wine, will lift our spirits. Thus, it offers us a chance to inject exhilaration into what may be the banal routines of everyday life. There may, however, be much back-breaking toil to gather in the wine harvest.

742 OLIVE GROVE

Olive trees are symbols of peace, purity and victory. An olive grove may evoke triumph over adversity, over family conflicts or inner strife. The dreamer may be looking forward to a period of creativity.

743 STILE

Climbing over a stile, like straddling a horse, is a common dream-image of sexual intercourse. The stile may also be seen as a gate between two worlds, presenting an invitation to surmount what might otherwise appear to be an obstacle to progress.

744 GARDEN

If the garden is seen as an image of spiritual harmony, the dream carries with it a reminder that the Garden of Eden is also a paradise lost. The garden includes the perhaps difficult process of self-discovery symbolized by the Tree of Knowledge, aspirations to immortality invested in the Tree of Life, and the carnal temptations offered by the serpent down

SEE ALSO
739: **Being lost in dense vegetation** p.22, **Tree** p.296;
744: **Garden of Eden** p.32

in the unconscious. Freud sees the garden as an image of the female genitals, with the dreamer perhaps facing all the additional anxieties and preoccupations evoked by a Garden of Eden.

As an urban creation, a **park (745)** may present dreamers with a "communal" conception of paradise. Progress to self-awareness and efforts to cope with feelings become a matter for a whole community.

746 TREE

Linking the Earth with the heavens, a tree is in many cultures a symbol of the cosmos. The roots draw on the depths of the unconscious, the trunk is the solid body and the branches reach up to the higher enlightenment of the heavens. The dream-image can evoke the Tree of Knowledge and Tree of Life at the heart of Eden or the cross on which Jesus was crucified, which is often called "the tree" – a symbol of sacrifice and redemption. The tree is also humankind's family, bearing the fruit of human civilization.

SEE ALSO
746: **Garden of Eden** p.32,
Forest or wood p.294

747 EVERGREEN TREE

Evergreens were associated in ancient mythology with the Garden of Eden's Tree of Life and subsequently the Christian Cross. As symbols of eternal life and resurrection, evergreens express a warning to be cautious with the unbridled instincts of the unconscious if spiritual growth is to be achieved. Although its use as a Christmas tree outside Germany caught on only in the 19th century, the **fir tree (748)** is now firmly linked to the celebrations of the birth of Jesus. The image may express strong feelings, positive or negative, about family celebrations.

749 OAK TREE

The oak symbolizes majesty and divine justice, offering dreamers a feeling of physical and spiritual protection. The oak is also a powerful symbol of male sexuality, a father-figure whom we recall as encouraging and comforting rather than imposing or formidable.

   Acorns (750) are a positive phallic symbol, a virile promise of potency, abundance and prosperity.

751 PLANE TREE

As the pre-eminent urban tree, often the one element of greenery in a sea of brick, steel and glass, the plane may remind dreamers to keep in touch with natural feelings and be wary of artifice and over-sophistication.

752 NUTS

Opened to enjoy their kernel, dream-nuts are likely to be symbols of the female genitals. A nut that proves hard to crack may also signify a problem difficult to solve.

The **walnut (753)** has a female sexual symbolism. In dreams, the walnut demanding care when being opened to extract the kernel may correspond to the tenderness that the lover owes to the loved one.

754 PALM TREE

Tropical palms are the quintessential dream-image of exotic living and luxurious self-indulgence. Palms grow with their roots near the water and their tops in the sun, making them a happy union of mother- and father-symbolism. Milk-filled **coconuts (755)** offer a symbol of ingenuous and uninhibited sexuality.

756 JUNGLE

As a more savage and untamed version of the forest, the jungle suggests in dreamers a deeper anxiety. Wild beasts, snakes, poisonous insects, strangling **creepers (757)** and **carnivorous plants (758)** evoke an uncontrollable mass of violent unavowed instincts lurking in the unconscious.

SEE ALSO
756: **Being lost in dense vegetation** p.22

759 BLOSSOM

Pink and white blossom are for dreamers a symbol of innocence and virginity. This can refer specifically to the female or, more generally, to an attitude of spiritual naivety. The image of blossom fluttering down to the grass can signify the passing of innocence.

760 FLOWERS

With their petals and pistil, flowers are a graphic symbol of the female genitals, their commonest meaning in dreams. However, flowers may also represent the soul, a dreamer's spiritual centre, and in this sense will often differ in meaning according to the symbolism of their hue – forceful if red, self-denying if blue, and so on.

   Wild flowers (761) add a sense of freedom and freshness to their sexual or spiritual significance. Dreamers picking wild flowers may be turning away from their partner.

762 LOTUS OR WATER-LILY

SEE ALSO
765: **Three**
p.333; 766:
Four p.333

The lotus or water-lily was regarded in the mythology of the ancient Egyptians as the primal flower, the source of creation. In Buddhism, the lotus is an image of the individual's spiritual development: rising from the muddy depths of ignorance, the consciousness finally opens to its full glory in the sun of enlightenment. Both associations may infiltrate a dream of the flower.

763 CHRYSANTHEMUM

The chrysanthemum is an autumnal flower and the disposition of its petals evokes the rays of the sun. For dreamers, the flower may suggest longevity and self-affirmation.

764 ORCHID

Taking its name from the Greek *orchis* meaning testicle, the orchid is a symbol of fertility. Its delicate beauty has also made it an image of perfection and purity, evoking in dreams poetic feelings of sensuality.

765 CLOVER

Evoking prosperity and comfort ("living in clover"), the little three-leaved plant may represent feelings of well-being and spiritual balance. A four-leafed clover is said to be a symbol of good fortune, perhaps revealing our optimism – or our over-reliance on the forces of chance.

766 SUNFLOWER

The sunflower turning always in the direction of the sun may be seen as a perhaps too ready submission to the guidance of another. But like the lotus, this flower is surely most often a positive image, expressing the dreamer's yearning for openness or spiritual insight.

767 CORNFLOWER

Their cool shade of blue being linked with spirituality, cornflowers may suggest calm reflectiveness. Cornflowers are also often preserved as dried flowers, an image that might suggest that the dreamer's faith has become dessicated.

SEE ALSO
766: **The Sun** p.374; 767: **Blue** p.341; 770: **Red rose** p.46, **White** p.341; 771: **Creepers** p.299; 772: **Social meals**, p.150

768 DAISY

Daisies are frequently regarded as the flowers of our childhood when we made them into bracelets and necklaces, both images of female sexuality. The daisy's appearance in a dream may express a desire for a pristine, childlike asexuality.

769 IRIS

In the iris, the swordlike leaves and tall stem add a male sexual symbol to the female bloom. The plant may evoke ambivalent sexuality, most often emphasizing the Animus archetype (see p.17), the masculine aspect of a woman.

770 WHITE ROSE

White roses symbolize the pure soul and virginity and may represent the dreamer's yearning for innocence. In the East, white is a traditional shade of mourning, so for some dreamers the image may be prompted by bereavement.

771 IVY

Ivy may express a persistent determination to continue with a difficult task. It may also stand for an unwelcome, even parasitical presence in your life – despite its seeming attractiveness, this presence may be subtly undermining your peace of mind.

772 HOLLY

Appearing at the time of year when Christians celebrate the birth of Jesus, the red berries that adorn the spiny leaves of the holly bush are traditionally said to represent the spots of blood on the crown of thorns – a reminder of Christ's sacrifice. This makes holly an ambiguous dream-image of joy and pain – as well as a symbol of communal or family festivity.

773 MISTLETOE

Now a pretext for kissing at Christmas, mistletoe was once endowed with healing powers and symbolized immortality and wisdom. Today, the dream is likely to reflect sexual desire, perhaps with overtones of holistic fulfilment.

774 CYPRESS

Typical of the Mediterranean landscape, the cypress is also common in cemeteries. As such it is a symbol of mortality expressing the hope of rebirth and continuity.

775 HEATHER

An emblem of the wild outdoors, heather is also a Freudian symbol of female pubic hair and likely to signify a desire for sex. **White heather (776)** is a talismanic symbol traditionally said to bring good fortune: as with the four-leafed clover, perhaps the dreamer is overly dependent on chance – or other people – to sort out his or her life.

777 FERN

Used decoratively, ferns bring the wilderness into the home. They may evoke in dreams a sense of tamed desires, of urges from the unconscious rendered more manageable in everyday life.

778 YEW

Its presence in graveyards links the yew with death, but its longevity and resistance to the elements also make it a symbol of immortality. The fine-grained wood of the English yew was tough enough to make both the archer's bow and the infantryman's shield.

779 DESERT

Far from expressing an image of desolation and sterility, the desert's vast expanse may represent to

SEE ALSO

775: **Moss** p.46; 776: **Clover** p.301; 779: **Sand** p.291, **Plains or prairie** p.306

dreamers an invitation to seek out the realities of life lying beneath the surface. Sterility is there only if men and women make no effort to use the desert as a space for reflection.

780 ISLAND

As a safe refuge, an island may symbolize the firm ground of the conscious mind, on which the dreamer prefers to stay rather than risk exploring the intimidating seas of the unconscious. By the same token, a dream of swimming to the island may express the desire to escape the discomforts of the unconscious for the more reassuring realm of the conscious mind.

781 PLAINS OR PRAIRIE

The open plains evoke the endless possibilities open to the dreamer's imagination, a prospect at once exciting and daunting. The dream challenges us to find the necessary courage and determination.

SEE ALSO
780: **Desert island** p.154,
The sea p.284

782 RIVER

As the Greek philosopher Heraclitus said, we can never step twice into the same river, since its waters are always being renewed. A river evokes life's ever-changing flow, a liberating image reminding us that constant change may be something strong and beautiful rather than something to be feared – a reality of eternal renewal as well as loss. A **stream or brook (783)** offers a similar symbolism, but is perhaps a gentler image of change.

784 RIVERBANK

Like the Jungian interpretation of an island, the bank may represent the safe ground of the conscious mind to which dreamers are struggling to return when swimming in the river of their unconscious instincts. Or a dream may place them on the bank contemplating, with confidence or anxiety, the waters of the inner self.

An artificial **embankment or levee (785)** may suggest a need to build stronger defences to avoid being overwhelmed by an unmanageable flood of unconscious urges.

786 PIER

As a point of departure, the pier may suggest that the dreamer is about to embark on an important new venture. A derelict pier may represent an abandoned project that you may be glad to leave behind. Approaching the pier aboard a ship, you may be preoccupied by an undertaking that is coming to an end. Bright lights and a brass band on the pier may signify a growing sense of relief that the project is near completion.

787 LAKE

Offering an evocative metaphor for the unconscious, the lake's murky depths are teeming with our latent urges, occasionally rising to the surface of our conscious mind. Dreamers may find themselves fishing, swimming, sailing or drowning in the lake as an expression of varying degrees of serenity or anxiety. For Jung, the lake, like the sea, is a symbol of the Great Mother archetype (see p.17). The tranquil surface of a **pond (788)** can evoke the deceptive aspect of our unconscious – the still waters that run deep.

789 BOG OR SWAMP

The earth saturated with water presents a particularly treacherous image of the mother. The bog or swamp with its apparently stable surface suggests your difficulties in trying to break free from a mother who stifles your independence. **Quicksand (790)** reveals the treachery of a seemingly firm surface of reality. Dreamers exploring the desert sands may need the help of experienced guides who know the terrain.

SEE ALSO
787: **The sea**
p.284; 781:
Sand p.291

791 TRENCH

The shelter that turned into a death-trap in World War I, a trench may express your fears that a present situation, at school or work or in your personal life, represents a false state of security. You may feel the best way to end the uncertainty is to confront the source of the anxiety. A trench may be a warning against passivity and the inflexibilty of "entrenched" views.

792 PIT

The pit can be an anxiety-filled symbol of female sexuality. The dream-image may be seen as a sexual trap for unsuspecting passers-by. Jungians prefer to see in the pit an image of unconscious urges, sexual and otherwise, to be explored with care.

793 VALLEY

Often flanked by orchards and vineyards, a valley is a symbol of abundance bringing together the fertilizing elements of earth and water. A valley may also represent the path to enlightenment.

A rugged, steep-sided valley, often with trees hugging its slopes and a

river running along the bottom, a **ravine or gorge (794)** presents a dangerous but exciting image of female sexuality. Whether you are a man embarking on a new relationship or a woman discovering her own sexual depths, you may want to clamber down the sides of the ravine to explore what lies below. You may anticipate that the sexual adventure will be rewarding, if you do not lose your footing.

The sheer immensity of a steep **canyon (795)** may present an overwhelming image of maternal domination. Safety may lie in acceptance – rather than feeling impotent, we could try just moving step by step to find a point where the walls are less closed in.

796 FIELDS

Dreams of fields with crops still to be harvested signify a plenitude of ideas waiting to be explored and turned to good use. Fields of farmland reduced to stubble suggest that the dreamer has reaped the benefit of current ideas and may want to prepare for a new crop. You might also just want to lie in the field and take time out, especially if the image is of a tranquil, flower-filled **meadow (797)**.

798 WHEAT

Wheat symbolizes the gift of life, the seed of humankind and the inexhaustible riches of nature. The image may urge dreamers to lead a full life so that they and others may benefit from their creativity. Drawing on Christian symbolism, the image of **grain (799)** represents life's renewal following death. Jesus told his disciples: "A grain of wheat remains a solitary grain unless it falls into the earth and dies; but if the grain dies, it bears a rich harvest."

800 GRASS

From a spiritual perspective, a dream of grass may focus on the symbolism of its shade, green, to signify for the dreamer life renewed and the infusion of refreshing energies. At the sexual level, grass may be a Freudian dream-symbol of pubic hair. A dream of **lying in the grass (801)** may express a simple desire to relax, or – like similar dreams involving soft moss, sand or water – to return to the comfort of the mother's womb.

802 HEDGE

Hedges may combine the female sexual symbolism of dense vegetation with the image of a wall or fence as a barrier that acts as both protection and constraint. The image of a hedge may suggest that you see a sexual involvement as a restriction on your freedom.

SEE ALSO

798, 799: **Bread** p.144, **Harvest** p.291; 800: **Plains or prairie** p.306, **Green** p.343; 802: **Walls** p.238

803 SPRING

A spring as the source of life symbolizes maternity, but also the purity of clear, clean waters. From a Freudian point of view, the dreamer may see the spring as gushing forth a joyful sexuality. A Jungian interpreter may see it as the origin of the inner life and spiritual energy – an image of the dreamer's soul.

804 WELL

The common dream of dropping an object into a well and listening for a splash in the darkness below may express a wish to make tentative contact with the urges latent in our unconscious. Drawing water from the well may express a desire to bring some of those unconscious feelings to the light. A well may also stand for the dreamer's most valued talents and inner resources; if you discover that the well is dried up or that you are otherwise unable to draw water from it, this may represent your fears of creative sterility, or your frustration that you have no current outlet for your talents.

SEE ALSO
803, 804, 805:
Water p.284;
805: **River**
p.306, **Ravine**
or gorge p.310

805 WATERFALL

A cascade of water brings together images of female and male sexuality, where the roar and foam of the tumbling waters may evoke the sensation of orgasm. The turbulent activity of a waterfall also presents a powerful image of change.

806 CAVE

Emerging from a cave into broad daylight may symbolize a journey of spiritual initiation. Conversely, descending into a cave may represent a desire to explore the unconscious. A cave is also an image of the womb, in which we may feel protected from the anxieties of the outside world.

ANIMALS

807 WORMS

Symbols of death and decay, worms may appear in dreams as undesirable intruders who may be stealing or slowly destroying the affections of a loved one. The worms may also signal an impending financial collapse. Worms in a corpse may symbolize life's continuity after death.

808 INSECTS

Insects, like many other small creatures, are frequently dream-symbols for small children. A dream of killing insects may be recalling a childhood hostility toward a brother or sister that may persist in adult life.

809 EARWIG

An old superstition that earwigs crawl into the ears of sleeping people earns these creatures a place among anxiety-symbols. A more reassuring interpretation sees the earwig as a bearer of secrets from a loved one.

810 WASP

Wasps building a nest under the roof, symbolic home of the dreamer's higher aspirations, may indicate the difficulties of spiritual progress. The problems may come from the skeptical depths of the unconscious: **wasp-stings (811)** signify for Jung a dangerous attack by the instincts. Traditionally more benign, bees symbolize the sweet rewards of persistence.

812 FLY

Flies evoke a common dream-image of persistence and relentless pursuit (in ancient Egypt, war heroes were rewarded with golden flies, proudly worn on a gold chain). They may represent nagging creditors, importunate admirers or unwelcome bores who insist they are your friends. The fly can also be a false man or woman of action, apparently always busy but in fact achieving little.

813 MOSQUITO

Mosquitoes may represent tormenting instincts from the unconscious, the waters where they breed. A symbol of irritation, the mosquito violates the intimacy of its victims and feeds off their blood.

814 MOTH

The image of a moth flying too close to a flame may signal that the dreamer – or someone close – is in the grips of a death-wish. More mundanely, moths flying out of clothes in the wardrobe may suggest old arguments, full of holes, needing to be renewed.

815 BUTTERFLY

The butterfly is a common dream-image of fluttering inconstancy. For Jung, however, this beautiful and

SEE ALSO
811: **Honey**
p.31, **Bees** p.32

delicate insect is nothing less than a symbol of the whole psyche – as it was indeed for the ancient Greeks, for whom *psyche* meant both "butterfly" and "soul". Emerging from its chrysalis, the butterfly is also a symbol of resurrection.

816 BAT

The bat is an image of blind folly and the demonic. Dwelling in the darkness that symbolizes the inner self, bats may suggest uncontrolled urges rising from the unconscious to plague our efforts at self-awareness.

817 AND 818 TOADS AND FROGS

The squat and warty companions of witches and sorcerers, **toads (817)** represent the darker impulses of the unconscious. **Frogs (818)**, on the other hand, represent resurrection and renewal, a symbolism inspired by the proliferation of their spawn. A person changing into a frog or vice-versa, like a fairy-tale prince, may express doubts about your own or someone else's identity.

819 BULL

Among the most potent of all the symbols of virility, a powerfully built bull often conveys barely-contained violence, yet it may also represent great

creative force. A **bullfight (820)** may suggest a need to control or harness fiery passions in order to further your aspirations.

821 COW

The cow is usually a serene and comforting symbol of motherhood and fertility. The cow's horns are frequently seen as an image of the new moon, evoking the satellite's symbolic femininity. However, milking a cow may suggest a dreamer's fantasy about incest with the mother, particularly as milk may represent semen.

SEE ALSO
821: **Milk** p.147

822 DEER

The graceful and delicate female of the species presents an archetypal dream-image of femininity in an innocent and timid form. For a female dreamer, the image may express a regression to psychic infantilism. The creature killed by a hunter or predator may symbolize an ideal spirituality being destroyed by base instincts.

823 AND 824 HARE AND RABBIT

The speed with which a **hare (823)** scampers about and "boxes" in the mating season have helped to earn the animal its madcap reputation. In many traditions, the role of the archetypal Trickster (see p.15) is taken by a hare, so a dream-hare may be pricking the bubble of the dreamer's pretensions. The **rabbit (824)** shares the hare's scatty and mischievous, tricksterish attributes, but adds its own symbolism of rampant fecundity, pointing to an overheated libido – or just a wish to procreate.

SEE ALSO
825: One
object into
another p.352

825 WILD BEASTS

Wild animals evoke for Freud people in an excited sensual state. They may also represent our animal instincts and repressed emotions that we may keep caged in the unconscious. Wild beasts may also symbolize our deepest fears, especially about death.

826 AND 827 FOX AND COYOTE

The contradictory facets of the fox's legendary personality of the **fox (826)** have earned this creature a place among the roll-call of Tricksters in many cultures. Like the **coyote (827)**, its canine cousin, the fox is seen as sly and cavalier, independent-minded and self-satisfied, inventive and destructive, witty and silly, audacious and timid. For dreamers with spiritual aspirations, these animals can represent both the daring of our ambitions and the self-doubt that disrupts our progress.

828 WOLF

The wolf can symbolize the savagery of uncontrolled impulses in our unconscious, threatening to destroy the dreamer's first fragile spiritual notions. Alternatively, however, the wolf, lone hunter in the night, may evoke the courage and nobility necessary to the dreamer's solitary quest for self-fulfilment.

829 TIGER

Lacking the nobility that is traditionally attributed to the lion, the tiger has become a more terrifying and aggressive dream-image of beauty and cruelty. It may symbolize the violent impulses stalking the jungle of our unconscious. Dreams that pit a tiger against a lion may suggest a son-father rivalry.

830 LION

The lion's proud and powerful presence evokes the dignity and other admired qualities of the father. A lion hunting or killing its prey may evoke for the dreamer the father's authoritarian tendency or his sexual dominance of a submissive partner. For the British, the lion is a national emblem and may evoke tribal instincts, a yearning to belong.

831 LEOPARD

The proverbial constancy of a leopard never changing its spots makes the creature a cautionary dream-image, suggesting that aggressive or otherwise unruly instincts cannot be overcome.

832 TURTLE OR TORTOISE

The turtle or tortoise projects an image of perseverance, common sense and longevity. The head emerging from its shell presents an obvious phallic symbol, just as the head retreating back into the shell may evoke cowardly surrender or sexual impotence.

833 PIG

Despite being among the most intelligent of farm animals, the pig is traditionally a symbol of gluttony, ignorance, egoism and filth. The animal may evoke the dark urges of our unconscious as well as anal fixations

inspired by the muck in which the pig wallows. Dreamers who have been social rebels (especially in the 1960s) may associate pigs with the police and other authority-figures.

834 GOAT

The goat has a disturbingly dual symbolism for dreamers. As a personification of the Devil, complete with horns and cloven hooves, unbridled libido and stinking breath, the image may evoke profound guilt-feelings about our sexual impulses. However, as the scapegoat sacrificed to expiate our sins, the goat has the sanctity of an innocent victim, whom dreamers know is being unjustly punished.

835 DOG

Dogs enjoy a universal symbolism as humanity's faithful companions and guides. But a vicious hound tearing apart a helpless prey symbolizes the assault of untamed instincts on the unsuspecting enterprises of our conscious mind. The **bulldog (836)** is an image of stubborn but good-natured pugnacity.

SEE ALSO
834: The Devil
p.349

837 CAT

The cat owes much of its dream-image to a reputation for being both gentle and sly. However, cats are also independent-minded and may be gentle only when it serves their purpose. Like the dog, the cat frequents the underworld of our unconscious, not as a faithful guide for lost souls but as an accomplice of witches hell-bent on letting unconscious urges get the better of our higher aspirations.

838 MOUSE

The mouse is an eminently sexual symbol, generally connoting pubic hair, but specifically male when imagined slipping in and out of its hole. A mouse caught in a trap can be an image of castration. Pounced on by a cat, the mouse may be seen as tentative first steps toward self-awareness falling victim to our baser instincts.

839 RAT

The image of rats rummaging around in the bowels of the earth can be at once phallic and anal. Dreamers may be suffering guilt-feelings, disgust, even pent-up rage about their sexuality. The anal fixation associated with rats may indicate a tendency toward avarice.

840 ROBIN

A traditional symbol of religious martyrdom, the little red-breasted bird may symbolize the innocent victim of an injustice.

841 PARROT

From the parrot's bright plumage and its talent for imitating human speech, the dream-image may evoke someone whose appearance attracts attention despite the person's inability to make a genuinely valuable contribution.

842 DOVE OR PIGEON

Interchangeably with the pigeon, the dove is a symbol of peace and reconciliation (as the bird that brought the olive branch back to Noah's Ark) and of love (the emblem of the Holy Spirit).

843 TURKEY

Associated with Thanksgiving and Christmas, the turkey may conjure up more or less happy family reunions. A bird too tough to carve may indicate more strife than harmony. An image of the carcass can suggest a wish to strip away all the family's hypocrisies.

SEE ALSO
843: **Social meals** p.150;
846: **White** p.341

844 DUCK

Ducks swimming in twos, often followed by ducklings, project an image of conjugal bliss. Japanese hotels put pictures of a pair of ducks in honeymoon suites – a custom now catching on in the West.

845 GOOSE

The goose is a symbol of marital fidelity. As harbingers of the changing seasons, geese flying in formation may signify an anticipated adjustment in the dreamer's personal or professional fortunes.

846 SWAN

The swan is a symbol of sexual desire, female in its pure white virginity, male with its long phallic neck. Hearing a swan singing – a swan has no song, but is said in legend to sing just before it dies – may be associated with bereavement or the end of a romance.

847 VULTURE

Vultures circling in the sky are a frequent dream-symbol of anticipated death. They may be awaiting with glee the outcome – perhaps (in dream interpretation) the conclusion of some enterprise – from which they expect to benefit. Devouring the flesh of the dead, vultures may also be regarded as a force for regeneration, drawing on vital energies from the past.

848 AND 849 MONKEYS AND APES

Monkeys (848) are often seen as a caricature of the dreamer's self, exaggerating and mocking any tendencies to be greedy, brutal or lascivious. However, the monkey may also project a positive, even ideal image – lively, free, agile and unpredictable – for dreamers yearning to escape a hidebound existence. In Buddhism, monkeys symbolize the restless, flitting mind.

Apes (849), such as chimpanzees, orang-utans and gorillas, frequently appear in dreams as stupid or clumsy versions of humans. But, as people in Borneo say, "if orang-utans do not talk, it is because they are too wise".

850 HORSE

The horse is a powerful dream-symbol of sexuality for Freudian interpreters, particularly if it is being ridden. Jungians see the horse as a symbol of nature's wild forces tamed by humankind. A winged horse, such as the mythical Pegasus, may symbolize energy unleashed for psychological or spiritual growth.

851 ELEPHANT

The elephant is often seen in dreams as being indifferent to pain, but by the same token insensitive to the feelings of others, wreaking havoc in situations that demand delicacy and tact. Owing to their apparent longevity, elephants may also be associated with the dreamer's grandparents, evoking perhaps the patience and wisdom of that older generation.

852 CAMEL

The slowly rocking, rolling motion of riding a camel is likely to evoke sexual intercourse. Spiritually, as a companion in the desert, the camel may become the dreamer's guide through vast expanses of arid speculation on the path to an oasis where insights can refresh the spirit.

SEE ALSO
850: **Prizes** p.25, **Horse-drawn vehicle** p.129, **Towpath** p.134, **Riding** p.134, **Horse race** p.174

853 SNAKE

The image of evil attributed to the snake may have its parallel in people's reluctance to accept the sometimes distasteful dream interpretations offered by Freud. The snake in the Garden of Eden and Freud in Vienna both present an idea that some find uncomfortable: that sexuality is not something to feel guilty about. Besides being an obvious phallic symbol, the snake embodies for Jung other "dark, incomprehensible and mysterious" aspects of the self that must be confronted.

854 CROCODILE

Floating half-submerged by the riverbank, the crocodile swims in the murky waters of our unconscious, projecting an image of voracity with its jaws and hypocrisy in its tearful eyes. A dream focusing on the crocodile's teeth may express a fear of castration.

855 SHARK

The shark is a terrifying symbol of death and destruction. Its open jaws may represent the female genitals in dreams of castration anxiety.

856 WHALE

Symbol par excellence of the womb, the whale may swallow Jonah (or the dreamer) in what for Freud expresses a grand act of incest and for

Jung a fear of being devoured by the mother. The whale regurgitating Jonah (or the dreamer) may express a resurrection or spiritual rebirth.

857 COD

While for Freudians all fish are phallic symbols, the dream-image of cod may acquire a domestic dimension as basic fare for lunch or supper. Dreamers may be yearning for what is perhaps a childhood memory of a simpler, more homely existence.

858 CRAB

Seeming to spread out in all directions with their evasive, sidelong gait, crabs are frequently associated in dream-symbolism with cancer (Latin for crab), whether real or imagined. With their habit of burrowing under the sand, they may represent anything sapping the dreamer's energy.

859 SHRIMP

Like other small creatures, a shrimp may represent a dreamer's childhood resentment toward a smaller brother or sister (for whom "shrimp" is often a disparaging nickname). Especially when coupled with the mother-image of the sea, the shrimp reawakens a dormant sibling rivalry.

SEE ALSO
855, 856, 857, 858, 859: **The sea** p.284

IMAGININGS

NUMBERS

860 ZERO

Standing alone in a dream, a zero is without substance or value and may express desolation. Appearing to the right of other numbers, a zero multiplies them by ten and thus takes on a sense of fertility and abundance – infinite potential rather than infinite void.

861 ONE

For Freud, numbers may reveal their meaning through each individual dreamer's free association. For Jungians, numbers represent "archetypal energies of the collective unconscious". One suggests harmony and union in a family or other group, but also an imposed uniformity, denying diversity. One can also represent the dreamer ("oneself") and symbolize the erect phallus, pointing to sexual issues.

862 TWO

SEE ALSO

862: **Pair of masks** p.80;

864: **Square** p.338

Two is the duality that permits movement, progress toward a truth, dialogue rather than monologue. Two may evoke interaction between the unconscious and conscious minds. It can be male and female,

father and mother, coming together and parting. Two is also ambiguity of meaning, doubt (being "in two minds") or ambivalence over some issue or person. In religious terms, two is the number of Christ, the perfect union of God and man.

863 THREE
Three completes the human being by uniting body, mind and spirit. For Christians, three represents Father, Son and Holy Spirit, but the number has sacred connotations in other cultures too. For Freud, three symbolizes the male genitals. Three can also reflect relationship troubles – "Two's company, three's a crowd."

864 FOUR
Four is said to express the essence of the material world – the four points of the compass, the four seasons, the four elements of water, air, fire and earth. As Jung's "quaternity" of the conscious and unconscious minds – thoughts, feelings, senses and intuitions – four can represent a moving forward to self-awareness.

865 FIVE
Five may symbolize our five senses and the five points of our body in harmony with the cosmos – feet planted on the ground, arms stretched

to the horizons, head communing with the heavens (represented in Leonardo da Vinci's celebrated image of the ideal man).

866 SIX

The number six may symbolize the universal struggle between good and evil, represented by the six-pointed alchemical star composed of two superimposed triangles, one pointing up to heaven and the other down to hell. Six is also the number of our psychic intuition, our "sixth sense".

867 SEVEN

A sacred number for many peoples, seven is the number of the rhythm of life and the passing of time (derived from the 28-day lunar cycle, divided into four seven-day weeks, and from the seven heavenly bodies known in ancient times: Sun, Venus, Mercury, Moon, Mars, Jupiter and Saturn). Seven stands for perfection and the completion of a phase of development. Life is said to run in seven-year cycles: in the West, adulthood is traditionally celebrated on the 21st birthday, and in Judaism a boy adopts adult responsibilities at the beginning of his fourteenth year.

868 EIGHT

Eight is a multiple of four and has a similar significance: wholeness or cosmic equilibrium and the complete integration of the psyche. Eight also symbolizes infinity or eternity, because apart from 0, the figure 8 is the only Arabic numeral to have no beginning or end.

869 NINE

As the number of months of human gestation, nine symbolizes the accomplishment of a creative task. As three times three, it has sacred significance as the number of total perfection and psychic balance. In Christian tradition there are nine orders of angels.

870 TEN

In the Jewish and Christian traditions, ten is the symbol of the law, the Ten Commandments governing the relations of human beings with each other and with God. As the sum of 1, 2, 3 and 4, ten is considered a perfect number integrating creation, movement, humanity and stability.

871 ELEVEN

Going beyond the law (represented by ten) and symbolizing incompleteness (the number of Christ's disciples after Judas' betrayal), eleven is a traditional symbol of transgression. St Augustine called eleven "the coat of arms of sin". Eleven can echo anxieties about a deadline – the "eleventh hour".

SEE ALSO
867: **STARS AND PLANETS**
pp.374–375

872 TWELVE

Twelve derives a religious significance from the twelve tribes of Israel and the twelve disciples of Jesus. In dreams, twelve may symbolize a vision of truth. Twelve months complete a life cycle in nature, prompting dreamers to prepare for the future.

873 THIRTEEN

The traditionally unlucky number thirteen – the number of the traitor Judas Iscariot, the thirteenth person at the Last Supper – causes anxiety for the superstitious. But it is also a symbol of optimism and completeness – the restored body of the original twelve apostles plus the apostle Paul. Thirteen focuses on the first month of a new annual cycle, bringing new hope. For many Mexicans, among others, thirteen is a propitious number, since their Precolumbian ancestors venerated thirteen gods and thirteen heavenly bodies.

874 THOUSAND

Symbolic of any vast number or expanse of time, a thousand may represent the immortality of love. Associated with a millennium and the coming of the Messiah, the number may be associated with any longed-for spiritual awakening.

SEE ALSO
872, 873, 874
Jesus Christ
p.58

SHAPES

875 CIRCLE

As an image without beginning and without end, a circle may be a symbol of perfection, time and eternity. A dreamer may find protection within the circle, often symbolized by a bracelet or necklace worn as a lucky charm, but an enclosing circle may also be a prison. For Freud, the circle represents the vagina. For Jung it is an archetypal image of the whole psyche, as opposed to the body, symbolized by the square.

A **sphere (876)** can share more fully the circle's symbolism of perfection. However, the image may evoke a spherical object – a breast, a testicle – suggesting a sexual preoccupation.

877 SQUARE

This presents the totality of the material world, as well as its limits, evoking the four restrictive walls of a house or castle. The square may express stability, but also stagnation and inhibition – having "square" attitudes. For Jung, images of a square within a circle, or the other way round, represent a rich balance of matter and spirit.

878 RECTANGLE

The rectangle may represent the Golden Mean, a geometric figure of ideal proportions symbolizing a harmonious relationship between the earth and the heavens.

879 TRIANGLE

The triangle gives form to the symbolic properties of the figure three: father-mother-child, Father-Son-Holy Spirit, and so on. The apex pointing up or down may represent respectively good or evil. For Freudians, the triangle is an image of the sexual organs, male pointing up, female pointing down.

880 SPIRAL

Evocative of staircases, snakes and entangling vines, the spiral is a symbol of sexual intercourse, but also of spiritual movement – toward our higher aspirations or our baser instincts. According to some interpreters, a spiral rotating clockwise may point to the higher ideals of our conscious minds, while a spiral rotating counterclockwise may indicate descent into the unconscious.

881 PYRAMID

Viewed by Freudians as a symbol of the erect phallus, the pyramid is a potent image. It may have a spiritual and aspirational significance for the dreamer similar to that of the famous Egyptian

SEE ALSO
875: **Ring** p.84,
Zero p.332;
877, 878: **Four**
p.333; 879:
Three p.333;
880: **Left
and right
side** p.64;
881: **Three**
p.333, **Four**
p.333

pyramid tombs for the pharaohs – a structure of mass and power that represented "material for eternity". The pyramid was a ramp that linked earth to the heavens, a beam of the creative power that was sunlight, set in stone and up which the deceased king would ascend to join the gods. The image may suggest the dreamer's effort to raise earthbound preoccupations (symbolized by the pyramid's square base) to a more elevated level, perhaps a striving after God.

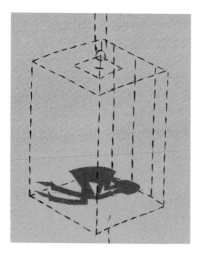

882 CUBE

A cube gives depth to the stability and completeness of the square. It may symbolize wisdom, truth and perfection, but a too-solid cube may evoke spiritual immobility. The cube may stand for a house, itself a symbol of the self. A person within a cube may represent the dreamer. In the form of a die, a cube expresses life's uncertainties – our subjection to factors beyond our control.

COLOURS

883 WHITE

As an absence of colour, white may evoke desolation or a bloodless corpse or ghost. White is the mourning shade of many Eastern cultures, such as China. More usually, white symbolizes purity and bridal virginity. As the light of dawn, white announces births and other beginnings.

884 BLACK

Black is the void out of which the universe was created and may indicate creative potential waiting to be brought to fruition. In many cultures, black also has traditional associations with death, evil and misfortune. If black stirs hostility for a dreamer of Caucasian descent, it may be a warning that deep-seated racial prejudices lie embedded in the unconscious.

885 BLUE

Blue expresses the sky's infinity and the sea's unfathomable depth. A lighter, celestial blue is the intellect, implying cool rationality, open-mindedness and steadfastness of purpose – if you have decided on a particular course of action, this may be a positive signal from the unconscious that you should trust your decision. A darker shade of blue may point more to the sea and the deeper regions of the unconscious. If you feel comfortable

SEE ALSO
883: **Zero** p.332;
885: **The sea
Water** p.284

with this hue, this could point to a readiness to liberate repressed feelings; if the shade prompts anxiety, those very feelings, repressed in this way, could be the root of any current "blues".

886 RED

This is the shade of anger and danger, the hue that says: "Stop!" But red is also passion and sexual desire and the traditional colour of devils and demons, which lurk in the unconscious to waylay our best intentions. Red's turbulent energy is not necessarily negative, for fire and blood are symbols of energy and life itself.

887 YELLOW

Bright yellow evokes the sun and the enlightened spirit. Yellow suggests dazzling insights, the shock of emerging from the dark into daylight. Pale yellow, on the other hand, smacks of sickness, decay, declining powers and old age.

888 ORANGE

Orange can be viewed as a balanced combination of the yellow of the spirit and the red of the libido: it can represent fertility or the dawning of spiritual awareness. In Buddhist countries the saffron robes of a Buddhist monk symbolize humility.

889 GREEN

Green is the symbol of spring, new life and awakening hope, as presented in leaves, grass or other fresh growth. However, as the hue of decay and death, green can reflect our pessimism or fear. "Green" can mean naive or immature, and its dream-presence may be prompted by an embarrassing occurrence that we may feel has revealed our inexperience. Green in a dream may also be provoked by jealousy, of which it is the traditional emblem.

890 BROWN

Brown may evoke earth as a source of fertility and rejuvenation, but brown also symbolizes the autumnal melancholy of rotting leaves. More significantly for Freudians, brown is the shade of excrement, indicating the anal fixation of an obsessively orderly character, together with miserliness – but also perhaps a repressed wish for artistic creativity.

SEE ALSO
886: **Fire** p.285,
Blood p.66;
890: **Toilet dreams** p.105

colours 343

SOUNDS AND VOICES

891 VOICES

Frequently heard detached from any identifiable people, voices may signify the inner self pressing to be heeded by a dreamer too concerned with everyday distractions. Voices of angels or some other kind of heavenly being may be a prompting from our higher spiritual self. Recognizable voices may remind the dreamer of friends or family who have been neglected.

Hearing a **call (892)**, as if from a great distance, may be a jog from the unconscious that someone we know is putting out distress signals. On the other hand, it may indicate that we should not be too proud to seek support from others when we need it.

893 BABBLE

At times of personal or professional stress, an unintelligible, but often angry-sounding babble may suggest barely controlled rage. It may need to be confronted and dealt with if it is not to erupt and wreak havoc in the dreamer's waking life.

SEE ALSO
891: **Angels** p.59; 893: **Inability to understand** p.51; 896: **Guns** p.47, **Artillery** p.183; 897: **Music** p.163

894 HEARING YOUR NAME

Hearing someone call your name may arise from some imminent occasion when you will be in the spotlight – such as a job interview or your wedding. If you are called by a name that is not your own, this may represent a side of your personality that you would rather repress.

895 WHISTLE

Whistles assert a person's presence or may be a signal to action. A whistle may be an affirmation of life, as in the old superstition of whistling as you pass by a graveyard.

896 GUNFIRE

Gunfire is associated with execution, warfare and crime. It may indicate a wish to get someone out of our way, such as a rival for promotion at work. A single shot, like the signal to a race, may reflect the pressure we feel while we are engaged on a project that needs to be completed by a fast-approaching deadline.

897 MELODY

A melody, whether familiar or not, may haunt a dream as an invitation to explore our perhaps neglected potential for personal creativity, of which music is a common symbol.

898 BELL

Evoking joy and festivity or mourning, church bells may reveal our true instincts. Thus, funeral bells might express our unspoken misgivings about a wedding. An alarm bell may be a simple reminder of something we have neglected.

899 DRUM

A drum-roll can symbolize the voice of our unconscious – unspoken feelings and instincts rumbling up from the depths of our inner self. A martial drum beat may evoke the rhythms of sex.

900 COCKCROW

The crow of the cock is an awakening, alerting us to new challenges. For Christians, the cock represents Peter's betrayal of Christ and may be a reminder that unforeseen events and emotions – especially fear – can test the integrity even of the most principled.

901 WHISPER

A dream-whisper may be our small but firm inner voice urging us to act in accordance with our instinct or, conversely, casting doubts on a firm resolution.

902 SHOUT

A shout can be a greeting or applause, perhaps for your performance of a difficult task. It may also be a warning, suggesting you should avoid acting too hastily.

903 AIR RAID SIREN

Commonly imagined by dreamers with memories of World War II, the wailing siren may express fears of the unknown, or a nostalgic longing for old comradeship and togetherness.

904 LAUGHTER

A sound of joy or relief, laughter may also express embarrassment or fear, perhaps revealing guilty feelings or (if others are laughing at us) a persecution complex or a sense of paranoia. Associated in folklore with wicked witches and mischief, **cackling (905)** may be our inner voice, ridiculing our pretensions.

906 FOUL LANGUAGE

Bad language and swearing often express anger or fear. The explanation may lie in a hitherto unexamined cause of resentment or anxiety.

SEE ALSO
898: **School bell** p.270; 902: **Fame** p.25

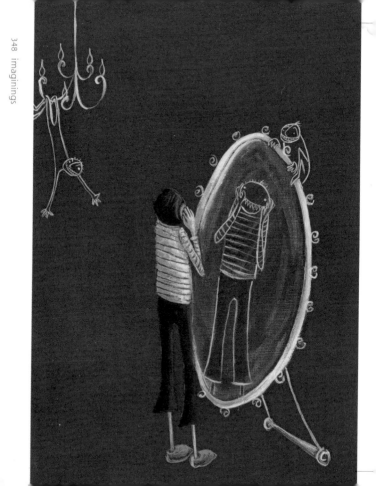

SPIRITS AND MONSTERS

907 THE DEVIL

The Devil may be seen as our dark unconscious and our disruptive baser urges. For Jungians, he could represent the Shadow archetype (see p.16). Dreams of the Devil may occur when we are contemplating a break with tradition that we expect may attract widespread disapproval.

Demons, imps, fiends and evil spirits (908) are often relics of unresolved childhood fears. They may be urges tempting us to transgress social norms, or may represent our dark side, our "inner demons".

909 MONSTER

Monsters may present in hideous form latent impulses that fill you with disgust. By giving these impulses a monstrous rather than human shape, you may be evading personal responsibility for them.

910 GIANT

Giants may appear in dream-replays of childhood memories, from a time when adults seemed so big to us. A brutal or scary giant may represent an intimidating parent.

911 FAIRY

Fairies may be of either sex but in dreams are commonly female. For Freud, they may express a

SEE ALSO
911: **Oedipus**
p.358

fantasy of incest with a female family member. A fairy in a man's dream may represent his Anima (see p.17) or, owing to its colloquial sense, repressed homosexual urges.

912 GHOST

The ghost of someone you know may represent "unfinished business" with that person. If unidentified, the figure may indicate lingering guilt from some "ghost" of the past.

IMPOSSIBILITIES

913 ABSURDITIES

Flying pigs, trains crossing the sea and other absurd or irrational images may signal your need to explore more creative approaches to life. An absurd scene may also represent your instinctive feeling that some situation in your waking life is fundamentally unworkable or unsustainable.

914 DISTORTED FACES

Unsuspected ambivalence about close friends or loved ones may be revealed in dreams that present them with repellently distorted features or bodies. Seeing yourself in this form may point to low self-esteem.

915 SUPERNATURAL DREAMS

For Jungians, dreams of supernatural events may be genuine transcendental experiences, offering a glimpse of the profound exaltation and peace at the core of our being. Freudians, though, see them as wish-fulfilling fantasies, expressing a desire to be free of everyday realities.

916 SEX-REVERSALS

If it does not express wish-fulfilment or simple curiosity, switching sex may suggest a need to cultivate your Anima or Animus (see p.17).

917 TALKING ANIMALS

Creatures that speak may signal a wish to draw upon the instinctual side of your nature. Not sharing human inhibitions, a talking animal may deliver an uncomfortable home truth that your conscious mind refuses to contemplate.

918 TALKING PAINTINGS

A painting or sculpture talking or coming to life may invite you to dissolve the bounds of inhibition (represented by the picture frame or the solidity of the sculpture's raw material). Is it time to animate the more creative, intrepid side of your personality?

SEE ALSO
912: **Symbols of death** p.108;
913, 918:
TRANSFORMATIONS
pp.352–353

TRANSFORMATIONS

919 ONE OBJECT INTO ANOTHER

Transformations often mean a wish to make changes, and the two objects involved can symbolize where our instincts are leading us. For example, a car turning into a house may point to a desire for a less mobile, more settled period in our life.

920 ANIMAL INTO PERSON

An animal transformed into a human suggests an urge to transcend primal instincts of which one may be ashamed. A hybrid sharing both human and animal traits, with, say, a bull's head and human body, may indicate the impossibility of divesting ourselves entirely of baser attributes – they may be best defused by self-acceptance, embracing the "beast" and acknowledging its part in our personality.

SEE ALSO
919: **Talking paintings** p.351;
920: **Minotaur** p.357; 922:
Trying to run p.29

The opposite transformation, of **person into animal (921)**, can express a desire to explore deeper levels of the psyche. If you work mainly with your brain, you may be hoping to make contact with more natural, spontaneous experiences.

922 PERSON INTO PLANT

Imagining yourself transformed into a plant or tree may suggest a wish to withdraw from the uncertainties of the human world. However, the dream may also be a warning against being "rooted to the spot", becoming stagnated or unwilling to break away from your fears. Conversely, a transformation of **plant into person (923)**, whether it is yourself or someone else, may evoke an awakening, a moment when inertia gives way to positive action in your life.

MYTH AND LEGEND

924 ZEUS OR JUPITER

As supreme deity in the Greco-Roman pantheon, Zeus (Jupiter to the Romans) is a father-figure in the full force of his powers, physical and mental. Wielding thunderbolts, he is uncompromising, ruthless when crossed, and sexually domineering. His formidable presence may evoke your anxiety in the face of your father or some other figure of authority.

925 DIONYSUS OR BACCHUS

The Greek god of wine and ecstatic transformations, Dionysus (Bacchus to the Romans) represents a heightened state of awareness, permitting us contact with our primal instincts and energies. Dionysus expresses the need to take risks if we dare to explore our full potential.

926 HERAKLES OR HERCULES

The ancient hero Herakles (Hercules to the Romans) represents the strengths and weaknesses of brute force. Depending on your circumstances, he might suggest the need for either a more robust or a more thoughtful approach to a problem.

SEE ALSO
926: **Hero** p.85;
931: **Distorted faces** p.350

927 APHRODITE OR VENUS

Aphrodite or Venus is the goddess of love and symbolizes a sexuality endowed with affection, encouraging us to be at ease with our bodies and sexuality. **Eros (928)** is the god of desire and sexual love, whose cherubic Roman form, **Cupid (929)**, presents the playful side of desire – and also the dreamer's pain when smitten by his arrow.

930 ARTEMIS OR DIANA

The Greek Artemis (Diana to the Romans) is a virgin huntress, proud, wild like the beasts she hunts, vindictive toward any who show her disrespect. She may evoke in women a wish to be more assertive and autonomous in their relations with men. In men, she may present the dominating, jealous and castrating mother-counterpart to Aphrodite.

931 MEDUSA

One of the three Gorgons of Greek myth, with snakes for hair above bulging eyes and a tongue lolling between fangs, Medusa's gaze turns people to stone. She may represent a distorted image of the self. Discovering destructive impulses without trying to understand and deal with them may petrify your efforts toward personal progress.

932 NARCISSUS

Narcissus is a handsome young man who falls in love with his reflection in a pool; when he tries to grasp the image he falls in and drowns, to be turned into a flower. The dream warns against vanity and narcissism, alerting us not to be preoccupied with mere appearances.

933 KING MIDAS

King Midas is granted the gift of turning to gold all he touches – including food, so that he almost starves. Midas suggests there are no short cuts to achieve the spiritual perfection symbolized by gold: we must draw on our own inner resources.

934 DRAGON

Fierce and fire-breathing, the dragon may be our Shadow (see p.16), the dark forces to address in our own nature if we are to achieve self-fulfil-ment – symbolized by the treasure that dragons often guard in legend. In the East, the dragon is fearsome but benign, represent-ing primal energy and the forces of heaven.

935 UNICORN

A pure white horse-like creature with a single horn on its forehead, the unicorn is tamed by a maiden who suckles it. In Christian legend, the maiden and unicorn symbolize the Virgin Mary impregnated by the Holy Spirit. Sublimating all carnal desires, the unicorn symbolizes a transcendental spiritual purity.

936 MINOTAUR

In the Labyrinth on the island of Crete, the monster with a bull's head and human body demands an annual sacrifice of maidens and youths until he is slain by the hero Theseus. The Minotaur evokes untamed impulses lying repressed in the unconscious.

937 JASON AND THE ARGONAUTS

Jason's voyage to find the Golden Fleece guarded by an unsleeping dragon admits of a classic Jungian dream-interpretation. Jason, the archetypal Hero (see p.16), must slay the dragon symbolizing his own dark impulses if he is to attain the spiritual purity represented by the Fleece. However, Jason only puts the dragon to sleep with a magic potion,

SEE ALSO
935: **Prizes** p.25; 936: **Labyrinth or maze** p.21; 937: **Prizes** p.25, **Hero** p.85

compromising his spiritual quest by leaving his impulses dormant and unconfronted. The quest for fulfilment demands total commitment.

938 HOLY GRAIL

The Holy Grail, said to be the cup from which Jesus drank at the Last Supper and which caught his blood at the Crucifixion, symbolizes spiritual perfection. Alone among King Arthur's Knights of the Round Table, **Galahad (939)** looks into the Grail, thanks to a spiritual purity denied to **Lancelot (940)**, who is too bound up in earthly concerns, principally his illicit love for Arthur's queen Guinevere.

941 SUPERMAN

The alter ego of the mild-mannered Clark Kent, Superman represents the classical qualities of the legendary hero. To fight evil and defend truth and justice, Superman remains sexually chaste, resisting reporter Lois Lane, to whom Clark Kent would happily succumb. We may feel guilty that such desire would distract us, as it did Sir Lancelot, from the quest for fulfilment.

SEE ALSO
941: **Hero** p.85;
944: **The sea** p.284

942 OEDIPUS

To prevent his predicted murder by a son, King Laius abandons Oedipus at birth. But Oedipus is saved by a shepherd and grows up to kill his father and marry his mother, both unknowingly. Figuring in the Oedipus complex fundamental to Freudian psychoanalysis, the legend has come to symbolize a man's hostility to his father and desire for incest with his mother. The female equivalent of the Oedipus complex is named after the mythical figure **Electra (943)**, who conspired to kill her mother Clytemnestra.

944 POSEIDON OR NEPTUNE

With his trident, symbol of lightning and tempests, Poseidon (Neptune to the Romans) is an unruly lord of the seas. He disrupts the deep waters of the dreamer's unconscious. However, his stormy, unpredictable temperament may prompt startling innovations in the dreamer's creativity.

945 HELEN OF TROY

The legend of Helen of Troy is a tale of two seductions. Greek daughter of Zeus who, disguised as a swan, seduced her mother, Helen is willingly carried off by Paris, son of the Trojan king. Helen's legend may suggest, with the ensuing war to retrieve her, the disastrous consequences of wanton self-indulgence and of male jealousy and pride.

Accepted by the gullible Trojans as a sacred offering, the giant, hollow wooden **Trojan Horse (946)**, in which the Greeks hide their soldiers to get inside Troy's besieged city walls, is a celebrated symbol of duplicity. The dream-image may reflect an obsessive fear that treachery lies behind an apparent act of generosity.

947 ACHILLES

Achilles, like Lancelot, is a flawed hero. The greatest of the Greek warriors in the Trojan War is also resolutely human, given to vindictiveness, ruthlessness, uncontrollable rage and childish sulks. These flaws have a physical counterpart in Achilles' heel, the one vulnerable part of his body. He may warn us to guard against complacency.

948 MAIDEN IN DISTRESS

Legends of a heroic knight rescuing an imprisoned maiden symbolize a courageous mind with strong convictions motivated by a quest for truth and honesty, symbolized by the maiden. Her imprisonment, classically by a wicked stepfather or other tyrannical male guardian, represents the repression of insights in the unconscious.

SEE ALSO
947: **Lancelot**
p.358, **Hero**
p.85; 949:
The sea p.284

949 MERMAID

This creature, half-woman, half-fish, is a symbol of sexuality and mystery. For the male dreamer she represents the Anima (see p.17), tempting him to explore the uncharted depths of his unconscious.

HISTORICAL FIGURES

950 PHARAOH

Associated in biblical tradition with inflexibility and persecution, the king of Egypt may symbolize the unbending authority of a father-figure.

The beautiful golden face of **Tutankhamun (951)** may recall the treasured delights of gilded youth; alternatively, the body embalmed for eternity may express a sense that we were denied the right to attain full maturity by our parents, especially – given the association with "mummy" – our mother.

952 JULIUS CAESAR

Caesar's assassins included Brutus, whom he is said to have regarded as a son – hence his dying words "Et tu, Brute!" ("Even you, Brutus!"). This famous scene may suggest our guilty sense that our hostility toward another, however justified, is nonetheless a betrayal. Caesar also warns against alienating others through overweening ambition and pride, whatever our talents. **Emperor Nero (953)** is an archetypal debauched and ruthless persecutor. Possibly the "Beast" referred to in the New Testament, he may possess in dreams the same symbolism as the Devil.

954 CLEOPATRA

The famous queen of Egypt combines sexual charm, political cunning and dynastic ambition to influence her powerful Roman lovers Julius

Caesar and Mark Antony. Ultimately dying by a self-inflicted serpent bite, Cleopatra presents a moral lesson about the perils of trying to balance love, power and ambition.

955 QUEEN ELIZABETH I

England's first Queen Elizabeth is seen both as a powerful female role model and as the Virgin Queen, renouncing sexuality for country. For Jungians, "Good Queen Bess" may evoke the archetypal Great Mother (see p.17), encompassing earthly powers and spiritual exaltation.

956 GEORGE WASHINGTON

Brave soldier and honest leader, Washington presents a prime image of the strong, protective paternal figure, the ideal "father of his country". Only Freudian fundamentalists would see in a dream-image of the legendary tree, which George admits to felling because he could "never tell a lie," our acknowledgment of illicit sexual feelings.

957 NAPOLEON

This paradoxical French hero, liberator and tyrant remains in the popular imagination as a symbol of the jumped-up dictator. Dreamers may see in him an overbearing father-figure.

SEE ALSO
953: **The Devil**
p.349

958 ABRAHAM LINCOLN

Lincoln may evoke the Wise Old Man archetype (see p.15), with its power to inspire personal growth and spiritual energy. He is a strong role model of justice, wisdom and compassion, to which his assassination (which he anticipated in a dream) adds the ultimate sacrifice of martyrdom.

959 ADOLF HITLER

The 20th century's ultimate villain, Hitler often appears in oddly casual encounters with the dreamer. This reminds us that dark urges are characteristics not just of fictional monsters but, far more disturbingly, of outwardly normal human beings. Jungians may see in him, and in the equally brutal **Stalin (960)**, the archetypal Shadow (see p.16).

961 WINSTON CHURCHILL

The greatest glory of Britain's wartime leader came when many believed his career to be over. Symbolizing dogged persistence and drive, he may be many people's ideal father-figure: tough and gruff but decisive, protective and courageous.

SEE ALSO
965: Maiden
in distress
p.360

962 JOHN F. KENNEDY

The dream-image of John F. Kennedy as dynamic, free-spirited archetypal Hero (see p.16) ennobled by martyrdom may be complicated by what we now know of his private life. But dreamers may feel more comfortable with such humanized heroism. A president is also a father-figure and JFK's publicized sexual appetites may be seen by some to enhance his virility. **Jacqueline Kennedy (963)** may appear as an iconic virtuous widow.

964 QUEEN ELIZABETH II

As a national matriarch, the current queen of England may represent the Great Mother archetype (see p.17), but her family troubles may have lessened the impact of this image. Dreams of social or sexual relations with this otherwise inaccessible figure express unrealistic fantasies or ambitions.

965 PRINCESS DIANA

Diana has become a symbol of the wronged and martyred heroine, but dreams may focus on her well-publicized acts of generosity and charity. Diana evokes the mythical image of the maiden held captive in a palace or castle symbolizing the constraints of social convention.

966 LEONARDO DA VINCI

The figure of an artist painting the Mona Lisa might evoke in the dreamer a desire to share the secrets of Leonardo da Vinci's multifaceted genius. Without seeking to emulate the Renaissance master, you may be trying to understand the mystery of the creative process.

967 MOZART

An ideal of the great artist who is tragically cut down at the height of his powers, Mozart also represents seemingly effortless beauty achieved through dedication and intense toil.

968 BEETHOVEN

Ludwig van Beethoven is the heroic artist who successfully challenges conventional forms in the face of profound adversity, in this case deafness – a fate so singularly cruel for a musician that it lends Beethoven's story an almost mythological dimension.

969 PICASSO

Dreamers often see Picasso in conjunction with one of his emblematic Cubist paintings in which he has broken down a face or body into its various facets. The dream-image may express a need to understand reality in its component parts, observe them separately, and then put them back together to understand reality as a whole. Picasso suggests the importance at least of observing life's complexity even if we cannot fully understand it.

970 THE POPE

The head of the Catholic Church may represent for many the archetypal Wise Old Man (see p.15), a benign and saintly father-figure. His intellectual and spiritual energy may stimulate us to raise our level of consciousness.

971 CARL GUSTAV JUNG

The appearance of Jung may reassure dreamers sharing his views of spiritual self-fulfilment that he is constantly present to steer them on their own quest for new insights. Jung may appear as a version of his own concept of the archetypal Wise Old Man (see p.15).

972 SIGMUND FREUD

Freud is both the founder of psychoanalysis and the classic image of the psychoanalyst, listening intently to the dreamer's anxieties. We may speak to the dream-analyst of things we keep from others and/or from ourselves. Freud himself believed that he turned up in his patients' dreams as a substitute for their own father.

BIBLICAL FIGURES

973 ADAM AND EVE

In Jungian interpretation, these sinful – or at best disobedient – figures play a paradoxically positive role in the unconscious mind. Adam and Eve become symbols of the "self-affirming ego". Together, they may be seen as the source of all our intellectual and spiritual independence. In the same vein, **eating the forbidden fruit (974)** from the Tree of Knowledge symbolizes a first step on the path to self-fulfilment.

975 CAIN AND ABEL

The archetype of fratricide and human strife, the murder of Abel by his jealous elder brother Cain symbolizes for Freud the rivalry between brothers and sisters for parental love. The dream may suggest that childhood animosities may persist unconsciously in adult life.

976 ABRAHAM

As the patriarch who breaks with idolatry to seek a more enlightened faith, Abraham symbolizes the dreamer's wish to depart from established conventional beliefs to find truths based on personal conviction. Abraham the nomad evokes the importance of exploring unfamiliar territories to find wisdom in depth of experience.

977 JACOB

Having tricked his elder brother Esau out of his birthright (another case of sibling rivalry), Jacob shows great courage by wrestling with an angel to win for his people the name and spiritual promise of Israel. Thus, he may stand for our higher aspirations.

978 MOSES

Moses is the bringer of the Law, who dies without entering the Promised Land, to which he leads his

SEE ALSO
974: **Apple** p.140; 977: **Ladder** p.116

liberated people from captivity in Egypt. He may symbolize the importance of moral integrity as a first step on the path to wisdom. The
journey – the process of learning – may in itself be even more valuable
than any final goal.

979 SAMSON AND DELILAH

Delilah destroys Samson's virility by cutting the hair that was the secret
of his strength. The dream evokes castration-anxiety and the self-
destructive dangers of an overheated libido.

FICTIONAL CHARACTERS

980 HAMLET

Freud saw Shakespeare's Hamlet as a version of the Oedipus complex of
latent hostility toward his father and desire for incest with his mother.
The prince hesitates to take vengeance on the usurp-
ing uncle who fulfilled Hamlet's own repressed
desire to kill his father and wed his mother.

Spurned by Hamlet, **Ophelia (981)** may symbolize a sexual partner regarded, albeit unconsciously, as a rival to the lover's own mother.

SEE ALSO
980: **Oedipus**
p.358; 981:
Sock p.50

982 MACBETH

Shakespeare's tragedy of the hero gone wrong, murdering his way to the throne, may suggest profound misgivings about our own or another's tactics of professional or social advancement. The witches' deceptive prophecies, which lead to Macbeth's downfall, reveal the dangers when ambitious people hear only what they want to hear.

Pushing her irresolute husband to act, **Lady Macbeth (983)** can appear less as a wife than as an archetypal domineering mother-figure. She may stand for our latent hostility or resentment toward our mother or any other influential woman in our lives.

984 ROMEO AND JULIET

The "star-crossed lovers" symbolize any relationship threatened because of family or other group hostilities. Dreamers may simply deduce that they need to exercise their personal judgment and not be influenced by social or peer-pressure.

985 CINDERELLA

The story of Cinderella competing with her sisters for the hand of Prince Charming may evoke sibling rivalry for paternal affections. Putting on the glass slipper that enables the Prince to identify his beloved is a Freudian symbol of the sexual act.

986 DON QUIXOTE

In his pursuit of lofty ideals with extravagant and outmoded chivalry, the foolhardy knight of Miguel de Cervantes' great novel embodies a warning to the dreamer to face life on realistic terms and not pursue unrealistic goals.

987 ALICE IN WONDERLAND

The tale of Alice is packed with symbols that may recall the first stirrings of childhood sexuality. Falling down a rabbit-hole into the earth, Alice may be seen returning to the womb. There she finds phallic symbols in the long ears of the **White Rabbit (988)**, the top hat of the **Mad Hatter (989)** and the Caterpillar on his mushroom.

990 PINOCCHIO

The puppet that turns into a little boy may evoke a wish to inject new life into stilted ideas. The phallic symbol of Pinocchio's nose growing each time he lies may represent guilt about sexual dishonesty.

991 SHERLOCK HOLMES

The great detective's relentless application of logical deduction in his search for truth may prompt dreamers to reject irrational mysticism in their own quest for philosophical insights.

STARS AND PLANETS

992 STARS

The stars may express an exalted identification with the universe or an accentuated sense of personal inadequacy. They may represent insights illuminating the unconscious. Ever-present in the northern-hemisphere night sky, the **Pole Star (993)** aids navigators and may act as a symbolic guide for those exploring the profundities of the cosmos.

994 SHOOTING STAR

The spectacular trajectory of a shooting star or meteor may represent a flash of inspiration or memories of someone deceased. Traditionally regarded as portents, **comets (995)** also evoke short-lived pleasures.

996 THE SUN

The blazing heart of the solar system, the sun is the source of creation and insight. An **eclipse (997)** suggests troubling events or emotions interfering with creativity or spiritual development.

SEE ALSO
996: **Parasol** p.263,
Summer's day p.283

998 THE EARTH

If we envisage the earth viewed from space we may be feeling emotionally insecure, adrift in a merciless universe. A dream of leaving the earth may arise from fear of death.

999 AND 1000 THE MOON
Dreamers may see the **full moon (999)** as a symbol of serenity or hope in dark times. A **crescent moon (1000)** may symbolize ambivalence.

1001 MARS
The planet on which humans have often hoped to find life may manifest our wish for close company, whether as individuals or as a species.

INDEX

ACKNOWLEDGMENTS

The publishers would like to thank the following illustrators for permission to use their work in this book: **Nick Dewar** pages 117, 233, 316–317, 340, 367; **Hugh Dixon** pages 16–17, 22, 59, 104, 244–245, 304; **Grizelda Holderness** pages 2, 65, 135, 181, 187, 222, 286, 292, 313, 326, 368; **Alison Jay** pages 85, 86, 91, 121, 128, 167, 176–177, 240, 252, 293, 336; **Peter Malone** pages 26, 34, 49, 72, 80–81, 108–109, 158–159, 169, 188, 207, 276, 342–343; **Sandie Turchyn** pages 124, 127, 235, 284–285, 356–357; **Heidi Younger** pages 75, 113, 193, 268–269, 321